Pocket Dictionary of Popes

Pocket Dictionary of Popes

Michael Walsh

BURNS & OATES
A Continuum imprint
LONDON • NEW YORK

Burns & Oates

The Tower Building, 11 York Road, London SE1 7NX
80 Maiden Lane, Suite 704, New York NY 10038

www.continuumbooks.com

This edition © Michael Walsh 2006

First published 2006

British Library Cataloguing-in-Publication Data
A catalogue record for this book is available from the
British Library.

ISBN 0–8601–2420–7 (paperback)

Designed and typeset by Kenneth Burnley, Wirral, Cheshire.
Printed and bound in Great Britain by MPG Books Ltd,
Bodmin, Cornwall.

Contents

Note to the Reader

Some years ago I edited a *Dictionary of Christianity Biography*. As well as the lives of the great and the good, this *Dictionary* naturally contained short lives of all the bishops of Rome (the popes), some of whom, a minority, were neither great nor good. The text which follows has been taken from that publication. All entries have, however, been revised, some of them substantially, and a handful of new ones added – the life of Pope Benedict XVI being an obvious example. As well as revising the entries, feast days of popes who are saints have been included in accordance with the day assigned in the latest calendar of saints. It is customarily, but not invariably, the date of death. A number of feast days were suppressed during the revision of the calendar – these have been noted. Some popes never made it all the way to canonization, and remained with the halfway title 'blessed'. Their feast days have also been mentioned. The place of a pope's burial is recorded where it is known. Many of the tombs are in either the basilica of St John Lateran, the cathedral church of Rome, or in St Peter's basilica on the Vatican hill, the shrine to the leader of the apostles. Many of these have by now disappeared. This is especially true for the tombs of popes who were interred in St Peter's. They disappeared when the original Constantinian basilica was knocked down and replaced by the present one in the course of the sixteenth and early seventeenth centuries.

Note to the Reader

The text of this book is arranged alphabetically, rather than being in chronological order. A chronological table of popes has been added immediately below. It follows the list of popes as it is to be found in the latest edition of the Vatican's yearbook, the *Annuario Pontificio*, though some of the dates differ slightly. The version printed here, however, includes in italics some of those regarded as antipopes by the *Annuario*, in most cases – though not all – because they were popes of either the Avignon or the Pisan obediences rather than the Roman one during the Great Western Schism (1378–1417). Where there is an antipope who had the same name as the accepted pope, that fact is indicated in the text. Italics are also used in the text for the lives of antipopes. Those dates marked with an asterisk (*) in the table indicate the date not of a death in office but of an abdication, sometimes a voluntary act, but most times not.

This is not a narrative history of the popes from Peter to Benedict XVI. There are several of these to be had, perhaps the best – certainly the most accessible to the general reader – being Eamon Duffy's *Saints and Sinners* (London: Yale University Press, 1997 – and since reprinted and updated). There are two standard reference works in English, J. N. D. Kelly's *The Oxford Dictionary of Popes* (Oxford: Oxford University Press, 1986 – again often reprinted and updated), and *The Papacy: An Encyclopedia* edited by Philip Levillain in three volumes (New York and London: Routledge, 2002), which is a revised version of the *Dictionnaire historique de la papauté*, first published in 1994. Although it has to be used with caution, Wendy J. Reardon's *The Deaths of the Popes* (Jefferson NC and London: McFarland, 2004) contains much interesting, and out-of-the-way, information.

A final note about dates. A good many of these are uncertain, especially in the first millennium. But there is a further complication. For much of the history of the church a pontificate was regarded as beginning with the pope's consecration rather than with – as now – his election. On occasion a pope died before he was consecrated. This was so in the case of Stephen II – hence the dual form of numbering of successive Pope Stephens. Sometimes both the date of the election and of consecration are known. Sometimes one or the other. Because of the necessity at one time of securing imperial approval for an election, there was often a long delay between election and consecration. In the chronological table I have tried to provide the date of election, where it is known, rather than that of a pope's consecration.

Chronological List of the Popes

Chronological List of the Popes

Chronological List of the Popes

Chronological List of the Popes

Lives of the Popes

Adeodatus I, the name later given to **Deusdedit** (see below).

Adeodatus II *born Rome, elected 11 April 672, died Rome 17 June 676.* Originally a monk, and during his papacy contributed greatly to the refurbishment of St Erasmus' monastery. A religious at heart, two letters are attributed to him in which he expresses his wish that monasteries be permitted to rely on internal jurisdiction only. He was an opponent of the Monothelite heresy. Buried in St Peter's, his feast is celebrated on 26 June though it is unclear whether he was ever formally venerated as a saint.

Adrian *see* **Hadrian**.

Agapitus I *saint, born Rome, installed 13 May 535, died Constantinople 23 April 536.* Agapitus was of a noble family, his father being Gordianus, a priest assassinated in 502. A student of both the Greek and Latin fathers of the church, Agapitus had hoped to found a college of scripture studies at Rome, but the unsettled conditions of the time made this impossible. A firm supporter of Chalcedonian faith, he would not allow Arians converted to the orthodox faith to rise to clerical office, despite the wishes of Emperor Justinian. He approved Justinian's document, already accepted by Pope John II, accepting as orthodox the Theopaschite formula that 'One of the Trinity suffered in the flesh', but added that laypersons were not permitted to become involved in matters of doctrine. He travelled to Constantinople for political reasons – to attempt to dissuade the emperor from invading Italy – but while there came into conflict with the patriarch Anthimus, who was sympathetic to Monophysitism. He died in Constantinople and on 20 September 536, after a funeral in that city, his remains were buried in St Peter's basilica. Feast day 22 April.

Agapitus II *born Rome, consecrated 10 May 946, died Rome December 955*. He was appointed pope by Alberic II of Spoleto (c. 905–54), 'prince' and effectively ruler of Rome. Nothing of Agapitus' earlier life is known. As pontiff he wielded political as well as ecclesiastical power and was particularly concerned with the promotion of monastic reform. It was Agapitus who granted Cluny its privileged status, and enlisted monks from Metz to come to San Paolo fuori le Mura in order that monastic discipline be restored. Though a man of great intelligence and diplomatic skill, the weakness of his position was demonstrated at Alberic II's death. Alberic on his death bed summoned the noblemen and clergy of Rome, requiring them to swear that Octavian – his bastard son – would become pope on Agapitus' death. The pope himself consented to this and on 31 August 954, Octavian became prince of Rome and then, following Agapitus' death, its pontiff. Agapitus was buried in the basilica of St John Lateran, Rome.

Agatho *saint, born Sicily, consecrated 27 June 678, died Rome 10 January 681*. Possibly from Palermo, he had been a monk, proficient in Greek as well as Latin. His election to the papacy was speedily ratified by the imperial exarch at Ravenna. He supported the Sixth General Council convened by Constantine IV Pogonatus in 680 against the Monothelites, at which was asserted, in explicit agreement with Pope Agatho's letters, the orthodox doctrine of two wills operative in Christ. His short reign was thus important for the abandonment of Monothelitism by the Byzantine government and the resultant reopening of amicable relations between the holy see and Constantinople. He upheld Bishop Wilfrid of York's appeal to Rome against the unexpected division of his see by Theodore, Archbishop of Canterbury, and restored him to York. He also furthered the spread of the Roman liturgy in England. He was a kindly man, loved by all for his cheerful good humour, and generous to his clergy even though he was desperately short of funds. Buried in St Peter's, he came to be venerated in the eastern as well as the western church. Feast day 10 January.

Alexander I *saint, born Rome, elected c. 109, died Rome c. 116.* Early accounts have him succeeding Evaristus as fifth in line from St Peter, but later convention reckoned him as sixth pope. According to Eusebius his reign lasted ten years. Nothing is reliably known about him, other than that he held a leading position in the Roman church. Feast day 3 May.

Alexander II *Anselm of Baggio, born near Milan, c. 1000, elected 30 September 1061, died Rome 21 April 1073.* He was sympathetic to the Patarenes, a reforming movement supported by Rome, which was strongly opposed to the simoniacal practices that kept ecclesiastical benefices in the hands of unworthy clerics. He became bishop of Lucca in 1057, and pope with the help of Hildebrand (Gregory VII), but without the approval of Henry IV, and opponents of his election prevented his consecration – which occurred immediately – taking place in St Peter's basilica: instead, it was held in the church of San Pietro in Vincoli. King Henry had an antipope, Honorius II, elected at a Basel synod. The schism was officially ended by the Synod of Mantua in 1064, but not definitively until Honorius' death in 1072. Unsuccessful in his efforts to heal the rift between east and west, the conquest of Muslim territory in Italy and Spain by his allies prepared the way for the first crusades. Alexander intervened to defend the Jews in southern France and Spain in 1263, and renewed the prohibition of Gregory I against their maltreatment. He blessed

William's invasion of England in 1066, and two of his legates presided over a great council of the British church at Winchester in 1070. He acquired considerable stature as pope and moderate reformer, and his qualities have become more widely appreciated in modern times.

Alexander III *Orlando Bandinelli, born at Siena, c. 1105, elected 7 September 1159, died Rome 30 August 1181.* A prominent canon lawyer in the school of Bologna, a cardinal in 1150, chancellor of the Roman church in 1153 and, as legate under Eugene III and Adrian IV, a strong influence on papal policy in Europe. Victor IV, an antipope supported by Frederick I Barbarossa, immediately opposed him, with the result that Alexander was consecrated at Ninfa, rather than in Rome. The schism lasted 17 years, during which time Alexander lived in France, returning only in November 1165. He became involved in the conflict between Thomas Beckett and the English king, and though embarrassed by the impetuous archbishop, he nevertheless imposed a penance upon Henry II for Beckett's murder. At the Third Lateran Council in 1179, over which he presided, the right of electing a pope was vested in a two-thirds majority of cardinals. He strongly encouraged the scholastic revival of the twelfth century; he sent missionaries to Scandinavia, and legates to France to check the growing influence of Albigensian doctrines. Buried in St John Lateran, where Pope Alexander VII commissioned Borromini to construct a monument.

Alexander IV *Rinaldo de Ienne, born Ienne, near Anagni, c. 1195, elected in Naples 16 December 1254, died Viterbo 25 May 1261.* A nephew of Pope Gregory IX, Rinaldo had been made a cardinal deacon in 1227, and cardinal bishop of Ostia in 1231. He had played little part in the government of the church, being preoccupied by the problems of the Franciscans, whose protector he was. Having been elected in Naples, he was immediately concerned with issues in southern Italy and Sicily. He was not politically adept, but was more successful with problems internal to the church, reopening discussions with the Byzantines over reunion of the churches, and encouraging the friars in their conflicts with the diocesan clergy. He failed to establish himself in Rome, and governed the church from Viterbo, where he is buried in the church of San Lorenzo.

Alexander V Pietro Philargia, born Crete, c. 1340, elected pope of the Pisan obedience 26 June 1409, died Bologna 3 May 1410. Born into a poor family and orphaned when young, he was brought up by the Franciscans and joined the order. He studied at Padua, Norwich and Oxford, then taught in Russia, Bohemia, Poland, Paris and Pavia – where he was professor of theology at the time of his appointment to the bishopric of Piacenza. He went as bishop to Vicenza two years later, and to Novara the year after that, finally becoming archbishop of Milan in 1402. He was made cardinal in 1405, and legate for Lombardy, but was discontented by the failure to end the Great Western Schism. He took a lead in calling the Council of Pisa in an attempt to end the schism, and was himself elected pope. The two other claimants, however, those of Rome and Avignon, retained some, though slightly diminished, support. He despatched Baldassare Cossa, the future antipope John XXIII, to capture Rome, which he did, and a group of Romans came to Bologna to submit to Alexander, but he died there unexpectedly. He is buried in Bologna, in the church of St Francesco.

Alexander VI Rodrigo Borgia (or, more correctly, Borja) born Valencia, c. 1431, elected 11 August 1492, died Rome 18 August 1503. A nephew of Callistus III, who made him a cardinal in 1456, and chancellor of the Roman church the following year. He secured his own election to the papacy largely through bribery, not unexpected in a family riddled with nepotism and favouritism, of whom nearly 20 kin or familiars were cardinals during his lifetime. A powerful clan, the Borgias tended to extremes of villainy and holiness: Alexander's uncle was personally austere, and his great-grandson, Francis Borgia, became general of the Jesuits, and was canonized. Alexander led a dissipated life, both as cardinal and pope, and through his nine illegitimate children, his blood now flows in many of the princely families of Europe. A capable administrator and a patron of the arts (Michelangelo created the *Pietà* for him), he encouraged the recitation of the Angelus, maintained a policy of tolerance towards the Jews (despite pressure to do otherwise), drew the boundary in the New World between the spheres of influence of Spain and Portugal and eventually prosecuted Savonarola for schism and heresy. He promoted the evangelization of Greenland, supported Portuguese missionary work and worked for peace between Portugal and Spain in the Far East and the Americas, as well as encouraging the spread of the gospel. Despite his positive contributions in many areas of the church's apostolate, any overall judgement of him and his pontificate will probably always be negative, even though the calumnies of his enemies have often been exaggerated. He was originally buried in the San Andrea rotunda, but in 1610 his remains were moved to the Spanish church, Santa Maria de Montserrat.

Alexander VII *Fabio Chigi, born Siena, 13 February 1599, elected 7 April 1655, died Rome 22 May 1667.* He served as nuncio at Cologne from 1639 to 1651, and was the papal representative at the Peace Conference of Munster. He refused to negotiate with heretics, and protested vehemently against provisions in the treaties he considered injurious to Catholicism. Elected in a stormy conclave that lasted 80 days, his position as pope was weak and he failed to establish good relations with Cardinal Mazarin, who had opposed his election, and had the support of Louis XIV of France. On the other hand, relations with Venice were more friendly. He was able to persuade the city to permit the return of the Jesuits in 1656, and lent it support against the Turks. As a theologian, Alexander had strong anti-Jansenist views, as did his predecessor, and when Antoine Arnauld, the Jansenist leader, proposed that, while the 'Five Propositions' were indeed wrong and one could accept the pope's condemnation of them, they were not to be found in Cornelius Jansen's *Augustinus*, Alexander made this subterfuge impossible in a bull stating that the 'Five Propositions' were in fact contained in *Augustinus*, and condemned them in the sense Jansen had meant them. A great patron of the arts, among his many projects in Rome he commissioned Bernini to enclose the piazza of St Peter's within the great colonnade. He is buried in St Peter's.

Alexander VIII *Pietro Vito Ottaboni, born Venice, 22 April 1610, elected 6 October 1689, died Rome, 1 February 1691.* Descended from a noble Venetian family, he entered the curial service and, named judge of the Rota (1643–53), became famous for his judicial decisions. A trusted collaborator of Innocent XI, Ottaboni was created a cardinal in 1652, grand inquisitor of Rome and secretary of the holy office. A complete contrast to his severe predecessor when elected to the papacy, but a jealous guardian of the faith, he condemned two laxist propositions current among Jesuits, one denying the necessity of an explicit act of love for God after the attainment of reason, the other admitting the notion of 'philosophic sin', i.e. a sin involving no offence to God because committed without knowledge or thought of him. He condemned in 1690 31 Jansenist propositions concerning penance, the virgin, baptism and the church's authority; also the 'Four Gallican Propositions' of 1682. He punished with life-imprisonment the surviving followers of the Spanish Quietist Miguel de Molinos; effected a reconciliation with Louis XIV who, in 1690, gave back Avignon and Venaissin, taken from Alexander VII. His reign was notable for generous aid to Venice in the Turkish wars; for extravagance in dispensing papal monies and offices, for his nepotism and for his patronage of the Vatican Library. He is buried in St Peter's.

Anacletus (Cletus) *saint, elected c. 80, died Rome c. 91.* His name is correctly Anencletus, a Greek adjective meaning 'blameless', and is probably to be identified with 'Cletus', a shortened form of the full name. Nothing is known of him, and while his existence and leading position need not be doubted, the fact that the monarchical episcopate had not yet emerged at Rome, makes it impossible to form any clear conception of his role. Feast day – suppressed in 1969 – 26 April.

Anastasius I *saint, born Rome, elected 26 November 399, died Rome 14 or 19 December 401.* On his election he plunged immediately into the controversy over Origen and his writings, particularly a translation of his *First Principles* by Rufinus of Aquileia, which had greatly offended Jerome in Bethlehem, and Jerome's influential circle of friends in Rome. Though Origen was only a name to Anastasius, and he had little grasp of the issues at stake, he condemned a number of Origen's doctrines on the strength of a letter received in 400 from Theophilus, the powerful patriarch of Alexandria. It dwelt on the evils caused by Origen's works, and reported their recent condemnation in Egypt. Rufinus then defended his work and his own theological position, and Anastasius, though sceptical about the motive behind Rufinus' translation, left him to God's judgment. Anastasius earned the praise of Jerome and Paulinus of Nola for his blameless life and apostolic solicitude. In other matters, Anastasius did not commend himself to the African bishops who, because of a shortage of clergy, wanted a relaxation of the ban on Donatist clergy returning to the church. Anastasius told them to continue the struggle against Donatism, advice the Africans tactfully ignored. Buried in the cemetery of Pontian. Feast day 19 December.

Anastasius II *born Rome, elected 24 November 496, died Rome 19 November 498.* The son of a priest named Peter, his election reflected dissatisfaction with the hardline attitude of Felix III and Gelasius I to the Acacian Schism (484–519). He sent legates to Constantinople exhorting Emperor Anastasius to help bring the Alexandrian church back to Chalcedonian orthodoxy, making it evident that he wanted peace and would make concessions, such as recognizing the baptisms and ordinations performed by Acacians. The emperor refused, however, hoping the pope would eventually accept the Henoticon, a superficially inocuous statement which made concessions to Monophysitism. Anastasius' efforts at reconciliation were misunderstood and created dismay among the Roman clergy, some of whom renounced communion with him and a schism threatened. At the height of the crisis, Anastasius suddenly died and with him possibly the last hope of reunion of east and west, on the basis of an orthodox interpretation of the Henoticon. Medieval tradition claiming that, as a traitor to the papacy who wished to restore the heretic Acacius, led Dante to consign Anastasius to the sixth circle of hell in his *Inferno*. He is buried in the portico of St Peter's, and his epitaph survives.

Anastasius III *born Rome, elected probably at the beginning of September 911, died Rome probably October 913.* Son of Lucian, and esteemed for his rectitude of life, little is known of his earlier career, or of his election and brief reign. He succeeded Sergius III, and ruled in a time of turmoil when Rome was dominated by Theophylact, consul and senator, and his ambitious, energetic wife, Theodora the Elder. This powerful and unscrupulous family effectively controlled the papacy. It is unlikely that, in such circumstances, the mild and unassertive Anastasius exercised any independent initiative. In 912 he received a letter from Nicholas I Mysticus, Patriarch of Constantinople, deploring Rome's attitude in approving Emperor Leo VI's fourth marriage in 906. No response survives, but Nicholas cannot have found it satisfactory, for he proceeded to remove the pope's name from the diptychs (the tablets with the names of the living and dead publicly prayed for at mass). Buried in St Peter's, an epitaph survives.

Anastasius IV *Conrad of Subura, born Rome c. 1070 (Subura was an area of Rome between the Esquiline and Viminal hills), elected 8 July 1153, died Rome 3 December 1154.* Nothing is known of his career until Paschal II appointed him cardinal priest of Santa Pudenziana c. 1112. In 1126 he became cardinal bishop of Santa Sabina and, in 1130, actively supported Innocent II in a divided election, proving himself a determined partisan, and an opponent of Anacletus II. He was elected pope on the day of Eugene III's death, and on 12 July enthroned in the Lateran. A very old man, he had much experience in curial business and had proved his abilities as vicar of the holy see in testing times. In matters of policy, he showed conciliation, and was criticized for being weak. He restored St William, who had been deposed by Eugene as archbishop of York, and thus closed a dispute over his appointment which had raged through four pontificates. Through the efforts of Nicholas Breakspear (Hadrian IV), Anastasius' legate in Scandinavia, both Norway and Sweden began paying 'Peter's Pence'. He is buried in the Lateran in the porphyry sarcophagus of St Helena.

Anicetus *saint, born Emesa (Homs) in Syria, elected c. 155, died possibly a martyr c. 166.* During his pontificate, St Polycarp came to Rome from Smyrna to urge the pope to adopt the practice of dating Easter on the fourteenth of the Jewish month Nisan, as did the churches in Asia Minor. It seems likely that a problem had arisen because of the diversity of the Christian communities in Rome. Anicetus responded that the church of Rome celebrated the resurrection every Sunday, and had no special Easter festival. Although they disagreed, Anicetus invited Polycarp to preside at mass. Feast day – suppressed in 1969 – 17 April.

Anterus *saint, Greek by birth, elected 21 November 235, died 3 (or 5) January 236.* He succeeded Pontian and was of Greek extraction. He died during the persecution of Emperor Maximus Thrax, though not necessarily as a martyr. He was the first to be buried in the new papal crypt in the catacomb of Callistus. Feast day 3 January.

Benedict I *born Rome, ordained bishop of Rome 2 June 575, died Rome 30 July 579.* Called Bonosus by the Greeks, he was the son of an otherwise unknown Boniface. The ravages of the Lombards made it very difficult to communicate with the emperor and Constantinople, whose confirmation was required before a pope could be ordained. However, the very long vacancy of over ten months may also have reflected problems among the clergy of the city as well as the military situation. Almost the only act recorded of him is that he granted an estate, the Massa Veneris, to Abbot Stephen of St Mark's 'near the walls of Spoleto'. From the few words the *Liber Pontificalis* has about him, it appears that Benedict died in the midst of his efforts to cope with the difficulties following the Lombard incursion. He is buried in St Peter's.

Benedict II *saint, born Rome, ordained bishop of Rome 26 June 684, died Rome 8 May 685.* A scripture scholar and a former member of the *schola cantorum*, he was elected in 683, but his consecration was delayed almost a year, awaiting the emperor's confirmation. During his term he amended the process of seeking this confirmation by having the exarch in Ravenna provide it. Benedict was greatly respected by Emperor Constantine the Bearded, who sent him locks of his sons' hair, making them the pope's spiritual sons. Benedict brought Macarius, the ex-patriarch of Antioch, back to orthodoxy from his Monothelitism, and restored several Roman churches. He upheld the cause of St Wilfrid of York, who sought the return of his see, from which he had been deposed by Archbishop Theodore of Canterbury. Feast day 7 May.

Benedict III *born Rome, elected July 855, ordained 29 September 855, died Rome 7 April 858.* The election of the learned and ascetic Benedict, son of Peter and cardinal priest of St Callistus, was a troubled one. On the death of Leo IV on 17 July 855 Benedict was chosen to succeed him, and envoys were sent to secure the ratification of the decree of ratification by the emperors Lothair I and Louis II. But the legates betrayed their trust in favour of the ambitious and excommunicated Cardinal Anastasius the Librarian. Most of the clergy and people, however, remained true to Benedict, and the legates had to yield. He was accordingly consecrated on 29 September (or possibly 6 October) 855. Because of dissensions and attacks from without, the kingdom of the Franks was in disorder. Benedict wrote to the Frankish bishops attributing much of the misery in the empire to their silence. He is buried in St Peter's.

Benedict IV *born Rome, elected (probably) January 900, died July/August 903.* Popes Benedict IV to IX inclusive belong to the darkest period of papal history; the reigns of several of them were very short. He was the son of Mammalus. His high birth, his generosity, his zeal for the public good, are loudly commended by the contemporary historian Frodoard, who gives him the title 'Great'. The principal act of his reign was his crowning of Louis the Blind as Emperor Louis III. He backed the decisions of Pope Formosus, who had ordained him priest, upheld the cause of Stephen, bishop of Naples, and excommunicated the assassin of Fulk, archbishop of Rheims.

Benedict V *born Rome, elected 22 May 964, died Hamburg 4 July 965.* The Emperor Otto I had forcibly deposed the unworthy John XII, and had replaced him with a nominee of his own, who took the title of Leo VIII. But at the first opportunity the Romans expelled Leo and on the death on 14 May 964 of the lawful pope (i.e. John XII), elected the cardinal-deacon Benedict. Otto was furious, marched on Rome, and put an end to Benedict's pontificate on 23 June 964. After reinstating Leo, Otto left Rome and carried Benedict with him to Germany. He was placed in the care of Adaldag, archbishop of Hamburg-Bremen, who treated him with great consideration; and he was even then acknowledged as pope by some of the German clergy.

First buried in Hamburg, his remains were later moved to Rome, though his tomb is unknown.

Benedict VI *born Rome, elected September or December 972, consecrated 19 January 973, died Rome July 974.* The son of a certain Hildebrand, he became cardinal deacon of St Teodoro. It was the necessity of waiting for the ratification of Emperor Otto that delayed his consecration as bishop. Nothing is known of his deeds, except that he confirmed the privileges of some churches and monasteries (his father is recorded as being a *monachus*, or monk). The most striking event of his pontificate was its tragic close. He was seized and thrown into the Castel San'Angelo by a faction of the nobility headed by Crescentius I and the antipope, a deacon named Franco who had styled himself Boniface VII. There, after a confinement of less than two months, he was strangled by a priest called Stephen on the orders of Boniface to prevent his release by Sicco, an imperial envoy sent to Rome by Otto II. The place of his burial is uncertain, but may be St Peter's.

Benedict VII *born Rome, elected October 974, died Rome 10 July 983.* Acting under the influence of Sicco (see entry for Benedict VI above), the Roman clergy and people elected to succeed Benedict VI another of the same name, the son of a certain David. The antipope Boniface VII opposed his authority and, though the antipope was himself forced to flee, his party followed fiercely in his footsteps and compelled Benedict to call upon Otto II for help. Firmly established on the throne by the emperor, he showed himself desirous of checking the tide of simony that was rising in the church, of advancing the cause of monasticism, especially in Germany, and of the conversion of the Slavs. He allowed St Majolus of Cluny to place his monastery under the special protection of the holy see, which helped to ensure the reform movement of the eleventh century.

Benedict VIII *Theophylact of Tusculum, born Rome (?), elected 17 May 1012, ordained 21 May 1012, died Rome 9 April 1024.* The son of Gregory Count of Tusculum and his wife Mary, he was still a layman when elected. He was a statesman of stature, and obtained the support of Henry II, whom he crowned emperor in Rome in February 1014. In 1016 the alliance of the pope, Genoa and Pisa successfully liberated Sardinia from the Spanish Saracens. He faced the most pressing problem of the church in his time, which was that of reform. The Ravenna Synod of 1014 issued decrees concerning ir-regular ordinations. The Synod of Pavia in August 1022 opened with an address by the pope. It decreed degrad-ation for non-celibate clerics in higher orders, and the reduction of their offspring to the status of slaves. The emperor approved these decrees, and enacted them as laws of the empire. He also encouraged monastic reform, especially under the influence of Odilo, abbot of Cluny, who had been present at the emperor's coronation.

Benedict IX *Theophylact of Tusculum, born Rome (?), elected 21 October 1032, deposed (for the third and final time) 16 July 1048, died Grottaferrata probably early January 1056.* The son of Alberic III, he was made pope at his father's behest when still a layman, and only some 20 years old. His life had been dissolute, and did not change after his election. Through he struggled fairly success-fully to free the papacy from imperial control, he was forced out of Rome in September 1044 by the popu-lace, who were wearied by his behaviour, and perhaps more by the domination of the Tusculani family. In March the following year, however, he regained power, but was prevailed upon to abdicate two months later by the offer of very large amounts of money. He retired to the family estates near Frascati. He returned, seemingly by popular demand – though more likely by bribery – in November 1047, only to be ousted again on the orders of the emperor the following July. In December he was excommunicated by a Roman synod for simony. He is buried in the abbey church at Grottaferrata.

Benedict X *John Mincius, born Rome, elected 5 April 1058, resigned January 1059, deposed April 1060, died 1073 or later. Son of Gui. Cardinal bishop of Velletri – and a reformer – at his election by a small group of Roman clergy wanting to control the papacy. He claimed at his trial, orchestrated by Hildebrand despite the fact he had willingly resigned in 1059, and that the office had been forced upon him. He was put under house arrest at Santa Agnese on the Via Nomentana, and lived long enough to see Hildebrand become Pope Gregory VII. He is buried at Santa Agnese.*

Benedict XI *blessed, Niccolò Boccasini, born Treviso 1240, elected 22 October 1303, died Perugia 7 July 1304.* He entered the Dominicans at the age of 14 and in 1296 he was elected master general of his order. As, at this time, hostility to Boniface VIII was becoming more pronounced, he issued an ordinance forbidding his brethren to favour the opponents of the reigning pope. When Boniface died, Niccolò was unanimously elected in his stead. The principal event of his reign was the restoration of peace with the French court. He was forced into exile in Perugia by the Colonna family, which then controlled Rome. He died suddenly in Perugia after a pontificate of only eight months. He is the author of a volume of sermons and commentaries on a part of the Gospel of St Matthew, the Psalms, the book of Job, and the Apocalypse. He is buried in St Domenico in Perugia. Feast day 7 July.

Benedict XII *Jacques Fournier, born Saverdun in the province of Toulouse 1285, elected at Avignon 20 December 1334, died Avignon 25 April 1342.* He studied at the University of Paris, where he received a doctorate in theology. He was abbot, in succession to his uncle, of the Cistercian house of Fontfroide, later bishop of his native diocese of Palmiers, and then bishop of Mirepoix, and was made cardinal of Santa Prisca, again in succession to his uncle, in 1327 by Pope John XXII. On the latter's death, during the conclave of 1334, he surprised the cardinals – and himself – by receiving the necessary two-thirds vote. He was enthroned on 8 January 1335. Resolved to re-establish the papacy at Rome, Benedict signalized his accession by providing for the restoration of St Peter's basilica, and for the Lateran. In the end he remained at Avignon, where he was responsible for the building of the massive papal castle that still survives. He was especially concerned for the renewal of the religious life, a concern which led him into conflict with the Cistercians, the Benedictines, the Franciscans and the Dominicans. His papacy was particularly noted for its economic probity and efficiency, which allowed him to give great quantities of money to the poor. He is buried in the cathedral church of Notre Dames des Domes, at Avignon.

Benedict XIII *Pedro Martinez de Luna, born Illueca, Aragon 1342 or 1343, elected pope of the Avignon obedience 28 September 1394, died Peñiscola 27 November 1422. He taught canon law at Montpellier. In 1375 he was made cardinal deacon, and he had the support of Castile and Aragon in favour of the antipope Clement VII, whose successor he became. He was deposed twice, first by the Council of Pisa on 5 June 1409, and then by the Council of Constance on 3 September 1417, but he had, in 1415, already retreated to Peñiscola where, in almost complete isolation, he adamantly maintained his papal* *claims until his death. He was noted for his knowledge of church law, and for his personal integrity: he had St Vincent Ferrer as his confessor. Six years after his death his remains were transferred back to the castle in which he had been born, but his tomb there was destroyed in 1811.*

Benedict XIII *Pierfrancesco Orsini, born Gravina di Puglia, Bari, 2 February 1650, elected 29 May 1724, died Rome 21 February 1730.* Against the wishes of his parents – his father was Duke Filippo Orsini – he entered the Dominican novitiate at the age of 16, taking the name in religion of Vincenzo Maria. On 22 February 1672 he was elevated to the cardinalate at the request of his family. In honour of the saintly Pope Benedict XI, also a member of the Dominican order, he took the name Benedict XIV, which he shortly changed to Benedict XIII, as Pedro de Luna (see above), who had previously borne the name, was a schismatic. In order to encourage the formation of diocesan seminaries he organized a special commission (Congregatio Seminariorum). At a Roman synod, held in the Lateran in 1725, he required an unqualified acceptance of the anti-Jansenist bull *Unigenitus*, and through his efforts Cardinal de Noailles, the archbishop of Paris, was persuaded to accept it in 1728.

Benedict XIV *Prospero Lambertini, born Bologna 31 March 1675, elected 17 August 1740, died Rome 3 May 1758.* In 1694, though only 19, he received the doctorates of theology and of *utriusque iuris* (i.e. of both laws, canon and civil). On the death of Innocent XII he was made consistorial advocate by Clement XI, and shortly afterwards a consultor of the holy office, and in 1718 secretary to the Congregation of the Council. He became bishop of Ancona in 1727, and a cardinal on 30 April 1728. Between 1708 and 1727 he was promotor of the faith, and in charge of canonizations, writing the classic study of the process. When Clement XII died on 6 February 1740 his fame was at its highest. Because of intrigues of various kinds the conclave which began on 17 February lasted for six months. To break the deadlock, Lambertini addressed the cardinals: 'If you wish to elect a saint choose Gotti; a statesman, Aldobrandini; an honest man, then elect me.' He was indeed chosen, and took the name of Benedict XIV in honour of his friend and patron Benedict XIII. As pope, Benedict XIV improved relations between the holy see and the states of Europe, both Catholic and Protestant. He engaged in reform of the church, especially of the clergy, and continued his own scholarly interests. This approach won him friends and admirers even among those otherwise hostile to Catholicism. *There was an antipope of the same name, 12 November 1425 (date of death unknown).*

Benedict XV *Giacomo della Chiesa, born Genoa 21 November 1854, elected 3 September 1914, died Rome 22 January 1922.* He studied law at Genoa and theology at the Gregorian University in Rome; becoming a doctor of sacred theology in 1879. He studied at the Academy of Noble Ecclesiastics, obtaining a doctorate in canon law in 1880, and became a lecturer there in diplomatic protocol. He thus entered the papal diplomatic service and soon caught the eye of Rampolla, later cardinal secretary of state to Pope Leo XIII, with whom he served at the papal nunciature in Spain. In 1901 he was made Substitute ('Sostituto' or deputy) secretary of state. Pius X made him archbishop of Bologna in 1907, though not a cardinal (despite the fact that the archbishop of Bologna is traditionally a cardinal) until May 1914. He was immediately faced with the problems arising from the First World War. He urged the United States' president Woodrow Wilson to use his great influence for a just peace, but expressed disappointment at the results of the Paris Peace Conference from which, at Italy's demand, the holy see was excluded. Benedict worked successfully to improve the holy see's diplomatic relations – in general he supported the League of Nations – and began the process which led, under his successor, to the settlement of the conflict between Italy and the papacy. His first encyclical put an end to the persecution of the Moderns. In 1917 Benedict promulgated the new Code of Canon Law, and his encyclical *Maximum illud* of 1919 urged missionary bishops to promote an indigenous clergy. He had a particular interest in the churches of the east, founding the Congregation for the Oriental Church, and the Pontifical Oriental Institute. He is buried in St Peter's.

Benedict XVI *Josef Ratzinger, born Marktl-am-Inn, Bavaria, 16 April 1927, elected 19 April 2005.* The son of a police inspector, he was obliged as a boy to be a member of the Hitler Youth, and then served briefly in the German army. He studied at Munich, completing a doctorate on St Augustine. He served as adviser to Cardinal Frings of Cologne during the Second Vatican Council, and afterwards moved to the University of Tübingen – from which he resigned as a result of the student riots of 1968. In 1977 he became archbishop of Munich, being created a cardinal the same year. In 1981 John Paul II asked him to come to Rome to head the Congregation for the Doctrine of the Faith, in which role he swiftly gained a reputation as a strict, though highly intelligent, enforcer of the Catholic Church's traditional teaching. By the time of John Paul's death he was dean of the College of Cardinals, and delivered the homily at the funeral mass. In the conclave which followed John Paul's death he was the early favourite, and gained a majority of votes on the fifth ballot. He soon made it clear that he would play a much less high-profile role than had his predecessor.

Boniface I *saint, born Rome, son of the priest Iocundus, elected 28 December 418, died Rome 4 September 422.* Having been the papal representative in Constantinople, he was ordained the day after his disputed election, when he was already quite old and frail. Because the prefect of the city supported the other candidate, Boniface was ordered out of Rome by the emperor Honorius, but his rival only succeeded in infuriating the imperial government, and Boniface was recognized on 3 April 419. He was indefatigable in promoting the authority of the papacy, and supported St Augustine and the other North African bishops in the controversy with the Pelagians. He is buried in the cemetery of St Felicity, on the Via Salaria. Feast day 4 September.

Boniface II *born Rome, though of German ancestry, elected 22 September 530, died Rome 17 October 532.* He was elected by a minority of the clergy: the majority, angered that the previous pope, Felix IV, had effectively nominated Boniface as his successor on his deathbed, elected Dioscorus. But Dioscorus died shortly afterwards, and Boniface was acknowledged by all as the rightful pope. He tried to re-establish unity by lavish gift-giving, but again alienated the clergy by attempting, unsuccessfully, to secure the election of a pro-German to the papacy to succeed him. He is buried in the portico of St Peter's.

Boniface III *born Rome, though of Greek ancestry, elected 19 February 607, died Rome 12 November the same year.* He had been created deacon by Pope Gregory I, who sent him as papal ambassador to Constantinople in 603. He established, and retained, very good links with the emperor in Constantinople who, at Boniface's behest, formally recognized the church of Rome as head of all the churches. Pope Sabinian had died over a year before Bonface's election. The delay in electing him was probably caused by rivalries in Rome, which may be why he issued instructions that there was to be no discussion of the papal succession during a pope's lifetime, nor for three days after his death. Buried in St Peter's.

Boniface IV *saint, born in the province of Valeria, Italy, elected 25 August 608, died Rome 8 May 615.* The son of a doctor, he became a deacon in Rome under Pope Gregory I and in 591 is mentioned as papal treasurer. During his pontificate he tried in many ways to emulate Pope Gregory. Like Gregory, he turned his home into a monastery. He also held a synod in Rome to regulate monastic life. This synod was attended by the bishop of London, to whom he gave letters for the English, for the king of Kent and for the archbishop of Canterbury. He received a letter of criticism from St Columbanus over his predecessor's behaviour in a doctrinal dispute, and obtained permission to turn the Pantheon into a church dedicated to the Virgin Mary. Buried originally in the portico of St Peter's, his remains were later moved into the basilica itself. Relics of the saint were later placed in St Mary in Cosmedin, and in the chapel of St Sylvester, in the church of the Quattro Coronati. Feast day 8 May.

Boniface V *born Naples, elected 23 December 619, died Rome 25 October 625.* Nothing is known of his early life except that he was the son of a certain John. He continued his predecessor's (Boniface IV's) interest in the conversion of England, but was more concerned with the prerogatives of the diocesan clergy, and less with those of monastic communities. He was described as 'compassionate and kindly', and distributed all of his personal fortune to the poor. Buried in St Peter's.

Boniface VI *born Rome, said to have been the son of a bishop, Hadrian, elected April 896, died in Rome the same month.* He had twice been degraded from the clerical state on charges of immorality, and his selection was forced upon the electors by a rioting mob. He was possibly murdered, though it is perhaps more likely he died of gout. He was buried in St Peter's, and an epitaph survives.

Boniface VII *named Franco, born Rome, elected June/July 974, died Rome 20 July 985. He was a cardinal deacon at his election, which was effectively a coup against Pope Benedict VI, the choice of the emperor Otto I. Benedict was imprisoned and Boniface consecrated. When the imperial representative in Italy, Sicco, hurried to Rome to overturn the appointment, Boniface had Benedict murdered in Castel Sant'Angelo. This act turned the people of the city against him, however, and he had to flee, taking the papal treasury with him. He returned to Rome in the summer of 980, in circumstances that are unclear, though he had to abandon the city again almost immediately when the emperor Otto II came to Rome at Pope Benedict VII's request. After the death of Otto he returned again in the pontificate of the unpopular Pope John XIV, who was deposed and subsequently murdered. When Boniface died unexpectedly – there were stories that he, too, had been murdered – his body was dragged through the streets and mutilated. There is no record of his burial place.*

Boniface VIII *Benedict Gaetani, born Anagni, Italy, c. 1235, elected 24 December 1294, died Rome 11 October 1303.* Born into a noble and influential family, Gaetani spent his early years serving the papal curia in minor capacities after studying civil and canon law in Bologna. He was created cardinal in 1281, played a role in the 1290 Council of Paris, helped to persuade Pope Celestine V to abdicate the papal throne, and was subsequently elected to fill the position. His almost nine-year reign was filled with conflict with both secular rulers (particularly Philip the Fair of France) and the powerful Colonna family, and with openly promoting his own family. Though he made a significant contribution to canon law, he was dogged by accusations of usurping the papal office and misusing it throughout his reign. That reign ended in 1303 when Philip's minister Nogaret seized the city of Anagni, where Boniface was, and from which he was about to excommunicate the king. Though he was not physically attacked, the encounter shattered Boniface's health, and he died several weeks later. He is buried in St Peter's.

Boniface IX *Pietro Tomacelli, born Naples, c. 1350, elected 2 November 1389, died Rome 1 October 1404.* An able ruler who succeeded Urban VI as pope of the Roman obedience and made notable progress in reversing the political and economic damage caused by his predecessor. The Jubilee of 1390 helped swell papal coffers, as did sharp financial practice. Renewed control of the papal states was not, however, matched by a resolution of the papal schism, which was fought out with his Clementine opponents in the parallel contest for the Neapolitan throne. Otherwise noted as a nepotist and as the pope who canonized Bridget of Sweden.

Caius *see* **Gaius**

Callistus I *saint, born Rome c. 153, elected 217, died Rome 222.* Originally, it seems, a Roman slave, he was then (according to Hippolytus) involved in some kind of fraudulent banking activities and was sent to the mines in Sardinia. Released at the request of Marcia, consort of Commodus, he was ordained by Pope Victor I, and subsequently became chief minister and successor to Pope Zephyrinus. He was attacked (unfairly) by Hippolytus for being a patripassian (i.e. believing that God the Father suffered in the sufferings of Christ), and for too lightly re-admitting to communion those found guilty of sexual misdemeanours. He was in charge of the catacombs on the Appian Way, which came to be named after him. He himself was probably martyred, possibly by being drowned in a well in Trastevere. He was buried first in the cemetery of Calepodius on the Via Aurelia. His tomb in Trastevere, to which his relics were transferred by Pope Hadrian I was excavated in 1960, is still venerated. Feast day 14 October.

Callistus II *Guido, son of William Count of Burgundy, born Quingey, France, c. 1050, elected in Cluny 2 February 1119, consecrated at Vienne five days later, died Rome 13 December 1124.* He became the archbishop of Vienne in 1088 and showed himself a prelate in the reforming tradition of Gregory VII. He was chosen as pope on 2 February 1119 by a small group of cardinal electors who were at the abbey of Cluny when Pope Gelasius II died there. Callistus was crowned at Vienne the week after his election. His election was not at first recognized in Germany, but when agreement to do so was finally reached, at the beginning of 1122, the pope used this opportunity to settle the struggle between the emperor and the papacy over control of the church – the 'investiture contest'. The Concordat of Worms of September 1122 carefully distinguished the spiritual authority of bishops from their temporal responsibilities, and while granting the emperor a say in the latter, denied him any rights over the former. Callistus also held the reforming First

Lateran Council in 1123. Buried in the basilica of St John Lateran.

Callistus III *Alfonso de Borja (Italianized as Borgia), born Játiva, Valencia, 31 December 1378, elected 8 April 1455, died Rome 6 August 1458.* A client of the Spanish antipope Benedict XIII and of the kings of Aragon, Borja became bishop of Valencia and a cardinal in 1444. During his brief pontificate the Christian powers rejected his calls to reconquer Constantinople, which had fallen to the Turks in 1453, though they scored a major victory against the Ottomans at Belgrade in 1456. Callistus was a notable nepotist, his nephew Rodrigo Borgia, the future Alexander VI, being most conspicuous among the many Spaniards who benefited from the pope's patronage. Callistus showed no interest in humanistic scholarship. Originally buried in the Rotunda of St Andrew, near St Peter's, his remains were later moved to the Spanish church in Rome, St Mary of Montserrat. *There was an antipope of the same name (1168–78).*

Callixtus *see* **Callistus III**

Celestine I *saint, born in the Roman Campagna, consecrated 10 September 422, died Rome 27 July 432.* The son of one Priscus, he was appointed a deacon by Pope Zosimus: his election as pope was apparently unanimous. In August 430 he excommunicated Nestorius, bishop of Constantinople, for his refusal to accept the title of 'Theotokos', or 'God-bearer' for the Virgin Mary, and sent representatives to the Council of Ephesus in 431 where Nestorius was again condemned. In Italy he took steps to deprive the followers of the heretic Novatian of their churches. He sent St Germain of Auxerre to Britain in 429 to convert the followers of

Pelagius and reputedly sent Palladius as the first bishop in Ireland. Buried in St Sylvester on the Via Salaria. Feast day 6 April, though the cult was suppressed in 1969.

Celestine II There are two popes with this title:

(a) *Teobaldo Buccapecus, born Rome, elected 15 December 1124, resigned the next day, and died shortly afterwards. Cardinal deacon of Santa Maria Nuova (c. 1103), cardinal priest of Sant'Anastasia in 1123, he was a very old man at his election. During the singing of the Te Deum a group of armed men broke into the church of St Pancras, where the election had taken place, and forced him to resign. Although he had already chosen the name of Celestine II, he had not yet been consecrated. While not an antipope, he is therefore not recognized officially as a pope.*

(b) *Guido di Citta di Castello, born Umbria, elected 26 September 1143, died Rome 8 March 1144.* A student – and friend – of Peter Abelard, he became cardinal deacon of Santa Maria in the Via Lata under Pope Honorius II. He served as a papal legate in many difficult situations, and the choice of Guido as pope reflects the need the cardinals felt for someone with considerable political skills. Contemporaries remarked upon his learning and his devotion. The most notable event of his short pontificate was the removal of the interdict which had been placed on King Louis VII of France by Pope Innocent II. Buried in St John Lateran.

Celestine III *Giacinto Bobo, born about 1106, elected, when still a deacon, in March or April 1191 at the age of 85, died Rome 8 January 1198.* Born into an influential Roman family, the son of Pietro Bobone. Appointed cardinal in 1144, he served the papal court for 44 years as cardinal deacon. A friend of Abelard – whom he had defended against St Bernard of Clairvaux – and of St Thomas Beckett. A learned and pious man, yet indecisive, his pontificate was dominated by the burgeoning power of Henry VI, whom Celestine crowned Holy Roman Emperor in 1191. Buried in St John Lateran.

Celestine IV *Goffredo Castiglioni, born Milan (?) c. 1187, elected Rome 25 October 1241, died Anagni 10 November 1241.* Of a noble Milanese family, his father Giovanni had married the sister of Umberto Crivelli, the archbishop of Milan who became Pope Urban III. Goffredo, thanks to this connection, rose through the ranks to be appointed cardinal priest of St Mark's in 1227 and cardinal bishop of Sabina in 1239. He was the first pope to be elected in a conclave, and was clearly chosen as a stopgap after 60 days of deliberation. He and the cardinals promptly left Rome for Anagni, where Celestine died only 17 days after his election.

Celestine V *saint, Pietro da Morrone, born about 1210, elected in Perugia 5 July 1294, abdicated 13 December 1294, died Castel Fumone 19 May 1296.* Of a peasant family – his place of birth is uncertain – he became a Benedictine monk (Pietro was his religious name) in 1232 at Santa Maria di Faifula, Montagno, possibly near his home village. He later lived a solitary life in the Abruzzi mountains, eventually founding a religious brotherhood, originally called the Hermits of St Damian (the name was changed to the Celestines on his election as pope). He was chosen after a vacancy of well over two years, partly at least as a result of a letter he had written at the instigation of the king of Sicily, Charles II of Anjou, upbraiding cardinals for the delay in choosing a pope. However, being 80 years of age, and under the influence of Charles of Anjou (who insisted on him remaining in Naples rather than Rome), and being politically and administratively naive, he resigned in December of the same year. His successor, Boniface VIII, held him prisoner in the castle of Monte Fumone until his death: there is some evidence that he was murdered. As Peter Morrone he was canonized in 1313. Feast day 19 May. Buried – after his body had been moved several times – in the church of Santa Maria di Collemagio, L'Aquila.

Clement I *saint, elected c. 90, died c. 98.* One of the early succession lists puts Clement as the immediate successor to Peter as bishop of Rome; others place him slightly later. In the first century, however, it is almost certainly anachronistic to call anyone bishop of Rome: Clement may have been one of the leaders of the Christian community in the city, and he achieved particular fame because of the *First Letter of Clement*, written by the Roman church to the church in Corinth, of which a certain Clement was said to be the amanuensis. He has been regarded as a martyr, though there is no evidence of this. Relics, said to be those of Clement, were found in the Crimea by Saints Cyril and Methodius in 868 and brought back to Rome where they were interred in the basilica of San Clemente. Feast day 23 November.

Clement II *Suidger, born 9 October 1005, elected Rome 24 December 1046, died, possibly of lead poisoning, Pesaro 9 October 1047.* He came from a well-to-do Saxon family. In 1040 he became bishop of Bamberg and in that capacity accompanied Henry III to the Synod of Sutri, where two of the claimants to the papal throne were deposed, and then on to Rome, where Benedict IX was likewise deposed. At the instigation of Henry, Archbishop Suidger was chosen, and the following day he crowned Henry as emperor. During his short pontificate he tried to enhance the authority of the papacy following the immorality and vice of Benedict IX. His reforms included the calling of the Council of Rome which condemned simony. He was buried at Bamberg.

Clement III *Paolo Scolari, born Rome, elected Pisa 19 December 1187, died Rome end of March 1191.* Son of Giovanni Scolari, he was brought up in Santa Maria Maggiore, of which he became archpriest, and eventually cardinal bishop of Palestrina. He came from a wealthy amd noble Roman family, and after his election he managed to settle the dispute between the commune of Rome and the bishop of Rome. Although in general a peacemaker, he promoted the third crusade for the recapture of Jerusalem from Saladin. He was responsible for the removal of the Scottish church from the jurisdiction of the Archbishop of York. He is buried in St John Lateran. *There was an antipope of the same name (1084–1100).*

Clement IV *Gui Foulques, born Saint-Gilles-du-Gard, near Nîmes in France c. 1195, elected 5 February 1265, died Viterbo 29 November 1268.* The son of a judge, he was himself originally a capable and successful jurist before he became a priest following the death of his wife. Bishop of Le Puy in 1257. In 1259 he became archbishop of Narbonne and cardinal bishop of Sabina two years later. He was elected pope in Perugia, though he was not present at the conclave. He lived in Perugia after the election, then moved to Viterbo, where he built the papal palace, because of unrest in Rome. He financed the invasion of Sicily and invested Charles of Anjou as king in 1266. He supported the work of the mathematician and philosopher, Roger Bacon. Buried now in San Francesco, Viterbo, but originally in the Dominican church of Santa Maria in Gradi.

Clement V *Bertand de Got, born c. 1260 at Villanddrout, Gironde, France, elected 5 June 1305, died Ropquemaure, Gard, 20 April 1314.* The son of Beraud, Lord of Villandraut, a territory then a fief of the English crown. After studying canon law in Orléans and Bologna he was appointed bishop of Comminges in 1295 and archbishop of Bordeaux four years later. He was elected pope in Perugia after a conclave of almost a year. Because of political disturbances in Rome, Clement settled in Avignon in 1309, bringing him under the influence of Philip IV. Thus commenced the 'Babylonian captivity' of the papacy which lasted until 1378. Under pressure from Philip, Clement suppressed the Knights Templar. Clement encouraged scholarship, founding the University of Perugia in 1307 and creating the chairs of Asian languages at Oxford and Paris. He promulgated the *Constitutiones Clementinae* in 1311, thus contributing to the development of canon law. In 1311 he convened the Council of Vienne.

Clement VI *Pierre Roger, born Maumont, Corrèze, France c. 1291, elected 7 May 1342, died Avignon 6 December 1352.* He was placed in the Benedictine monastery of La Chaise Dieu by his parents and, after a brilliant academic career, became abbot of Fecamp in Normandy. He became bishop of Arras, then archbishop of Sens, and finally archbishop of Rouen. He then entered the papal curia at Avignon, and was appointed cardinal in 1338. He centralized church finances, bringing them directly under the control of the papacy. He was criticized for the luxuriance of his court and his practice of nepotism. However, he displayed uncommon charity and philanthropy during the period of the Black Death (1348–50). He was a protector of the Jews, welcoming them to Avignon. He was buried in the monastery of La Chaise Dieu where his tomb survives, though his remains were burnt during the French wars of religion.

Clement VII *Robert of Geneva, born Annecy 1342, elected 20 September 1378, died Avignon 16 September 1394. The son of Count Amadeus III of Geneva, Robert joined the Franciscans, was educated at the University of Paris, and was successively bishop of Thérouanne and Cambrai before being made a cardinal in 1371. He was used on various diplomatic missions, and was in charge of the papal army sent in 1376 to pacify the Romagna. In 1378 he was among those who voted for Urban VI, but rapidly regretted the promotion of so unstable a character. Dissident cardinals declared Urban's election void and, having moved to Fondi, elected Robert in his stead. He was chosen unanimously, with only the three Italian cardinals abstaining. Related both to the French royal house and to the emperor, he was an obvious choice. Eventually taking up residence in the papal enclave of Avignon, he replicated the administrative machinery of the Roman curia and enjoyed the support of France, Burgundy, Naples, Savoy and Scotland, while England and the empire remained loyal to Urban. Urban's death in 1389 offered an opportunity to end the schism, but his cardinals elected Boniface IX to succeed him. Clement considered military action to seize Italy, but this came to nothing, possibly because of its cost: when he inherited the title of Count of Geneva he was forced to use his own funds to support a papacy impoverished by the schism. Originally buried in Notre-Dame-des-Doms at Avignon, Clement's remains were later moved to the chapel of the Celestines.*

Clement VII *Giulio de' Medici, born Florence, 26 May 1468, elected 19 November 1523, died Rome 25 September 1534.* He was the illegitimate son of Giuliano de' Medici and therefore a nephew of Lorenzo il Magnifico. He became archbishop of Florence from 1513, and cardinal, when his cousin became Pope Leo X and he ruled his native city on behalf of Leo. During his pontificate, Italy was convulsed by war, Clement being a mere pawn in French and imperialist hands. In 1527 imperial troops besieged the pope in Castel Sant'Angelo and sacked the city of Rome. After the siege of Castel Sant' Angelo was lifted Clement took refuge in Orvieto. In such circumstances, he was not well placed to respond to either the Lutheran threat in Germany or to King Henry VIII's demand for a divorce from Catherine of Aragon – who was, unfortunately for the pope, the aunt of the emperor. Despite all these vicissitudes, however, he remained an important patron of the visual arts. Though originally buried in St Peter's, his remains were later moved to the church of Santa Maria Sopra Minerva.

Clement VIII *Ippolito Aldobrandini, born Fano, Italy 24 February 1536, elected 30 January 1592, died Rome 5 March 1605.* He studied at Padua, Perugia and Bologna, and rose somewhat inconspicuously through the ranks of the papal curia before becoming cardinal in 1585. He was personally very devout, and close to the Oratorians in Rome. He was influential in the conversion of Henry IV of France to the Roman church, in the weakening of Spanish dominance of the papacy and in establishing the Treaty of Vervins in 1598, thus establishing peace between France and Spain. He appointed the future saint Francis de Sales as bishop of Geneva in an attempt to bring the Swiss back into Catholicism. His many reforms included the publication of revised editions of the Latin Vulgate, the Breviary and the Missal, and the extension of the Vatican library. He is buried in Santa Maria Maggiore.

Clement IX *Giulio Rospigliosi, born Pistoia 27 January 1600, elected 20 June 1667, died 6 December 1669.* He was made cardinal in 1657 in order to be secretary of state under Pope Alexander VII, having been governor of Rome under Alexander's predecessor Innocent X. His pontificate was characterized by efforts to achieve reconciliation between France and Spain, by the rise of Gallicanism and by a policy of appeasement towards the Jansenists. He was originally buried in St Peter's, but his remains were later moved to Santa Maria Maggiore.

Clement X *Emilio Altieri, born Rome 12 July 1590, elected 29 April 1670, died 22 July 1676.* A member of an old Roman family, he began his career as a lawyer, but later took holy orders and became bishop of Camerino in succession to his brother. Appointed as cardinal in 1669 by Clement IX, he had not yet received the red hat when he was elected. For someone who was almost 80 on becoming pope, he had a surprisingly active pontificate. He was troubled by the advance of Turkish forces, and gave financial support to John Sobieski, the future king of Poland, to oppose them. He was firm against the growing influence of Gallicanism, but was unable to improve relations with either France or Spain. Buried in St Peter's.

Clement XI *Giovanni Francesco Albani, born Urbino 23 July 1649, elected 23 November 1700, died 19 March 1721.* He was made cardinal in 1690 and was known for his scholarship, acquiring several important additions to the Vatican library, including manuscripts from the east. He made the feast of the Immaculate Conception a holy day of obligation in 1708 and issued two bulls, *Vineam Domini* (1705) and *Unigenitus* (1713), against Jansenism. He was unsuccessful in intervening in the events leading up to the War of the Spanish Succession (1701–14). Buried in St Peter's.

Clement XII *Lorenzo Corsini, born Florence 7 April 1652, elected 12 July 1730, died 6 February 1740.* The son of Bartolomeo Corsini and Elisabetta Strozzi, he belonged to an influential Florentine family, and when he came to Rome to study he lived with an uncle who was already a cardinal. After further studies in Pisa he moved to Florence before returning to Rome in 1685 and starting a career in the papal curia. Became cardinal priest of Santa Susanna (and later of San Pietro in Vincoli) in 1706 and was a patron of the arts. Despite constant ill health (possibly due to diabetes: he went blind in 1732, and from 1737 suffered from a loss of memory) he tried to re-establish the authority of the papacy, especially against the encroaching power of France. He condemned Freemasonry and encouraged missionary activities. Buried in St John Lateran.

Clement XIII *Carlo della Torre Rezzonico, born Venice 7 March 1693, elected 6 July 1758, died 2 February 1769.* His family was a member of the Venetian nobility through his mother, Vittoria Barberigo, and he was educated by the Jesuits at Bologna and became a doctor of law at Padua. He then entered the Academy of Noble Ecclesiastics in Rome, thus embarking on a career in the papal administration. He became cardinal deacon of St Nicola in Carcere in 1737, bishop of Padua in 1743, and cardinal priest of Santa Maria in Ara Coeli in 1747. His pontificate was dominated by the problem of the Society of Jesus. Following their expulsion from Portugal, France, Spain, Naples and Parma he resisted pressure from all over Europe to suppress the order. He was also concerned with the well-being of his subjects in the papal states, and greatly fostered piety in the church, particularly encouraging devotion to the Sacred Heart. He is buried in St Peter's, in a tomb designed by Antonio Canova.

Clement XIV *Giovanni Vincenzo Antonio Ganganelli, born Sant'Arcangelo, Italy, 31 October 1705, elected 18 May 1769, died 22 September 1774.* Educated by the Jesuits and Piarists, he became a Franciscan in 1723, taking the name Lorenzo. He taught theology and philosophy at convents in Ascoli, Milan and Bologna, writing a defence of the Jesuits (1743). He came to Rome in 1740 as regent of the Franciscan college, and wrote a treatise defending the Jews against traditional accusations. He was made a cardinal in 1759, though he never played a major part in the Sacred College. His pontificate was dominated by pressure from several European powers to suppress the Jesuits, which eventually he did in 1773 with the brief *Dominus ac Redemptor*. The story that during the conclave he had agreed to do so as a condition of his election is probably untrue.

Cletus *see* **Anacletus**

Conon *born Thrace (?, certainly of Thracian descent), elected 21 October 686, died 21 September 687.* Son of an army officer, he was educated in Sicily and ordained priest at Rome. He was elected pope as a compromise figure, in lieu of candidates favoured by the clergy and the military respectively. Already old and in poor health, he proved a somewhat gullible leader: his mistakes included the appointment of Constantine of Syracuse to administer the holy see's patrimony in Sicily. He was the recipient of a letter dated 17 February 687 from Justinian II stating that the decrees of the third Council of Constantinople had been endorsed by the Byzantine clergy. He is buried in St Peter's basilica.

Constantine *born Syria (?), elected 25 March 708, died 9 April 715.* The son of a certain John, he became archdeacon, and in that capacity attended the third

Council of Constantinople in 680–1. He then became papal ambassador to the Byzantine court. He was the last pope to accept as a matter of course the authority of the emperor in Constantinople. The *Liber Pontificalis* describes his visit to the east in 710–11, where he was warmly received by Justinian II at Nicomedia. When Justinian was assassinated in December 711, Constantine refused to recognize his successor, Philippicus (though he was soon deposed and replaced by an orthodox candidate, Anastasius II). Constantine authorized the English monastery of Bermondsey and Woking to choose its own abbot in 713, and he received the professions of the Mercian king Cenred and the East Saxon prince Offa at Rome in 709. Buried in St Peter's. *There was an antipope of the same name (767–768).*

Cornelius *saint, born Rome, elected 6 or 13 March 251, died June 253.* After the martyrdom of Fabian under Decius in 250, the see of Rome was vacant for 14 months, before an election could be held. Cornelius faced strong opposition from the supporters of Novatian, who had directed the church in the meantime. The Novatianists objected to his fairly lenient policy towards those who had lapsed during the persecution; however, the majority of bishops supported him. Several of his letters survive, including two to Cyprian. Exiled under Gallus' persecution, he is said to have been martyred at Centumcellae (Civitavecchia). He was, however, buried in Rome near the catacomb of Callistus on the Appian Way: an inscription has been found. Feast day 16 September.

Damasus I *saint, born Rome (?) c. 305, elected 1 October 366, died Rome 11 December 384.* He was of Spanish descent and the son of Antonius, who became a bishop. Damasus became a deacon and was ordained priest under Pope Liberius, whose successor he became. He was elected by a majority of the Roman clergy, despite violent opposition from a rival, Ursinus, and his supporters. He was also backed by the civil authorities of the city, in the hope that he might be better able to maintain peace. He was a staunch opponent of heresy, especially Arianism; he also did much to consolidate the strength of the church of Rome, promoting local martyr cults and building churches. He did much to enhance the authority of the Roman see. In his old age, he commissioned Jerome to commence a revision of the Latin Bible, a project which laid the foundations of the Vulgate version. He was first buried in the catacomb of Callistus, but his remains were transferred in the ninth century to San Lorenzo in Damaso, the church which the pope and his brother had constructed out of their father's house. Feast day 11 December.

Damasus II *Poppo, born Bavaria, consecrated 17 July 1048, died at Palestrina 9 August the same year.* He was bishop of Brixen, in the Tyrol, a see he kept even during his short pontificate. He was part of the entourage of the emperor Henry III during his visit to Italy in 1046, and stayed on to play a part in the Roman synod of 5 January 1047. This may have encouraged Henry to think of him as pope on the death of Clement II, though Poppo appears to have been unenthusiastic. Because of support for the antipope Benedict IX, he was for several months prevented from entering Rome. His choice of name indicates a desire to return to the imagined purity of the early church, but his ability to impose a programme of reform was never tested. Buried at San Lorenzo Fuori le Mura, where his sarcophagus can still be seen.

Deusdedit (Adeodatus I) *saint, born Rome, elected 19 October 615, died 8 November 618.* The son of Stephen, a subdeacon, he had previously served as a priest in Rome for 40 years. Deusdedit was pope during turbulent times, as the Byzantine army mutinied because it had not been paid. During his reign he had to contend with earthquakes and plague. Deusdedit favoured the diocesan clergy as opposed to monks, who had risen to prominence in the church under his predecessor. Deusdedit later became known as Adeodatus I. Buried in St Peter's. Feast day 8 November.

.

Dionysius *saint, elected 22 July 259 or 260, died Rome 26 December 268.* Dionysius is one of the most significant bishops of Rome of the third century. He reorganized the community, and called a synod which condemned both the Sabellian and Marcionite tendency of dividing the Trinity into three hypostases. Dionysius also assisted Cappadocian communities which had been devastated by foreign invasions. Feast 30 December.

Dioscorus *born Alexandria (?), elected 22 September 530, died 14 October the same year. He was a deacon in Alexandria, but fled the city for theological reasons and came to Rome where he played a prominent role in the clerical life of the city. He went as papal ambassador to Constantinople, and was suggested for the sees both of Alexandria and Antioch, but returned to Rome where he was elected by the pro-imperial faction. Boniface II was elected at the same time. His death shortly afterwards put an end to the schism in the Roman church, and he came to be regarded as an antipope, though there is no real reason for this.*

Donus *born Rome, elected 2 November 676, died Rome 11 April 678.* The son of a certain Maurice, nothing is known of him before the pontificate, and little enough of that. He was the recipient of a vague but conciliatory letter from Theodore, patriarch of Constantinople, seeking an end to the Monothelite controversy. Emperor Constantine IV Pogonatus also sent a conciliatory letter, but Donus died before he received it. Donus rebuilt and decorated several churches, including putting a marble pavement in the atrium of St Peter's, and disbanded a Nestorian monastery. Buried in St Peter's.

Eleutherius *saint, of Greek ancestry, elected c. 175, died Rome c. 189.* He was bishop of Rome in the reigns of Marcus Aurelius and Commodus. His tenure of the bishopric probably coincided with the heresy of Montanus, and of Basilides, Valentinus, Cerdo and Marcian, although exact dates are difficult to place. Letters from Irenaeus to Eleutherius deal with these matters, and Irenaeus also visited him in Rome. Said to have been buried near the tomb of St Peter. Feast day 26 April.

Eugenius I *saint, born Rome, elected 10 August 654, died 2 June 657.* The son of Rufianus, Eugenius was brought up in the church's ministry from childhood. As an elderly presbyter he was elected pope after the deposition of Pope Martin I by Emperor Constans II. The main theological issue of his reign concerned the nature of the will of Christ. Eugene had the reputation of a conciliatory pope, dispatching envoys to Patriarch Peter (654–66) at Constantinople. In 655 they agreed a new communion, affirming two natures in Christ, each having one will, yet also affirming that when Christ was a person he possessed only one will. The Roman people rejected the theological compromise and schism once again broke out. Buried in St Peter's. Feast day 2 June.

Eugenius II *born Rome (?) elected 5 June 824, died 27 August 827.* Eugenius was the cardinal priest of St Sabina, enthroned as pope by co-emperor Lothair I. Lothair, who had come to Rome to investigate crimes committed under the pope's predecessor Paschal I, established a new 'constitution' governing Rome, according to which all Romans, laity as well as clergy, should take part in papal elections, and that the pope, once elected but before his consecration, should take an oath of loyalty to the emperor. This constitution was ratified in a Latgeran synod in November 826. During his pontificate iconoclasm arose anew. Despite pressure from Emperor Louis the Pious, who sent a group of theologians to investigate the issue, Eugenius insisted on upholding the decrees of the Second Council of Nicea, which had approved the veneration of images. Buried in St Peter's.

Eugenius III *blessed, Bernardo Pignatelli, born Pisa, elected 15 February 1145, died Tivoli 8 July 1153*. Possibly prior of a house in Pisa, he met and was much influenced by St Bernard of Clairvaux. He subsequently became a Cistercian monk at Clairvaux and then abbot of Saints Vincent and Anastasius. In 1145 he became the first Cistercian to be elected as pope, although possibly not a cardinal. Between 1146–8 he was forced into exile due to his refusal to accept certain political reforms in Rome, and because of the opposition of Arnold of Brescia. Eugenius promoted the second crusade and authorized Bernard of Clairvaux to preach it: they both incurred hostility when it failed. He reformed clerical morality and monastic observance. Buried in St Peter's. In 1872 his cult was approved by Pope Pius IX. Feast day 8 July.

Eugenius IV *Gabriele Condulmer, born Venice c. 1383, elected 3 March 1431, died Rome 23 February 1447*. The early career of this Venetian patrician was moulded by the patronage of his uncle Pope Gregory XII. As pope he continued the work of Martin V in re-establishing papal authority in Rome and the papal states, but

Roman hostility drove him into exile in Florence (1433–43), where the curia offered employment to leading humanists. He was a tenacious anti-conciliarist, the Council of Basel in its schismatic phase going so far as to 'depose' him. The Ottoman threat to Constantinople prompted the Byzantine emperor John VIII Palaeologus to seek the help of the west. Eugenius called an ecumenical council at Ferrara and Florence, to which the emperor came in great state, which achieved reconciliation between the Greek and Latin churches. This detente proved to be short-lived. Buried originally in St Peter's, his body was shortly afterwards moved to the monastery of San Salvatore in Lauro.

Eusebius *saint, of Greek origin, elected 18 April 310, died Sicily 21 October the same year.* Eusebius, who was the son of a doctor, and possibly even a doctor himself, succeeded Marcellus I and immediately became embroiled with Heraclius in the controversy regarding the *lapsi*, who claimed the right to be received back into ecclesiastical communion without submitting to penance. Emperor Maxentius exiled both Eusebius and Heraclius to Sicily, where the pope died. His body was brought back to Rome and buried in the catacomb of Callistus. Feast day 17 August.

Eutychian *saint, born Luni, Tuscany, elected 4 January 275, died Rome (?) 7 December 283.* Limited details of his life survive, perhaps because of the Diocletian persecution, which followed shortly after his death. He himself, however, ruled the church at Rome at a relatively trouble-free period, and seems to have brought stability and organization to the Church, evidenced in the expansion of official Christian cemeteries at the time. Buried originally in the catacomb of Callistus, his remains were later moved to the abbey of Luni in

Sarzana, Italy, and after that to beneath the altar of Sarzana cathedral. Feast day 7 December.

Evaristus *saint, elected 99 (?), died c. 109, probably on 26 October, probably in Rome.* The *Liber Pontificalis* states he was of Greek ancestry, as well as giving some unreliable data about his pontificate; but no certain information survives. His usual designation as martyr is unproven. Possibly buried on the Vatican hill, near the tomb of St Peter. Feast day 26 October.

Fabian *saint, born Rome, elected 10 January 236, died (a martyr) 20 January 250.* He appears to have been influential politically, negotiating a previously unknown level of peace and social tolerance for the church. A respected leader, he reorganized the administration of the church's charitable activity by dividing the city into seven regions (the civil administration had 14), each in the charge of a deacon. He also appears to have created the orders of subdeacons, acolytes, porters and exorcists. Fabian's life was brought to an end when Emperor Decius renewed persecution against the church upon his accession. He was buried originally in the catacomb of Callistus, but a sarcophagus apparently containing his remains were discovered in 1915 at the church of San Sebastiano. Feast day 20 January.

Felix I *saint, born Rome, elected 3 January 269, died 30 December 274.* Few details survive. However, events in the east, surrounding Bishop Paul of Samatosa, make it clear that already in Felix's pontificate not only was the authority of the bishop of Rome significant in the church at large, but even the emperor, who referred to the bishop of Rome as an arbiter in a dispute over churches, recognized it. Feast day 30 May.

Felix II appointed by the emperor Constantius, late 355, died near Rome 25 November 365. He was the archdeacon of Pope Liberius, and had sworn an oath, when Liberius was exiled, to remain loyal. However, he travelled to Milan where he was consecrated bishop by Arian bishops at the emperor's instructions, and then returned to Rome where he had a number of followers. Liberius' return in 358 led to clashes between the two factions, which effectively Felix lost, withdrawing from the city to an estate just outside.

Felix III *saint, born Rome, elected 13 March 483, died Rome 1 March 492.* He was the son of a priest, also called Felix, and had been married: his wife and children were buried in the basilica of San Paolo fuori le Mura. Felix was the great-great-grandfather of Pope Gregory. The pope sent an embassy to Constantinople to persuade the emperor not to give his support to the anti-Chalcedonian patriarchs of Alexandria (Peter Mongos) and Constantinople (Acacius). His legates, however, were taken in by Acacius, and Felix excommunicated both Acacius and his legates. The excommunication was reciprocated, thus causing the first schism of the eastern and western churches. He also excommunicated many Catholics who had been forcibly rebaptized by Arian Vandals. Buried, with his family, in San Paolo fuori le Mura. Feast day 1 March.

Felix IV *saint, born Samnum (near modern Benevento), elected 12 July 526, died Rome 22 September 530.* A 58-day gap between Felix and his predecessor, Pope John I, suggests a struggle for the papacy; Felix was consecrated on the orders of Theodoric, the Ostrogoth king of Italy. In the controversy over semi-Pelagianism he wrote 25 propositions concerning grace, largely taken from the writings of St Augustine via a collection made by Prosper of Aquitaine, which were adopted at the Second

Council of Orange (529). As he lay dying he bestowed the pallium on his archdeacon, Boniface, thus designating him as his successor. Boniface did indeed succeed him, though only after the brief pontificate of Dioscorus. Buried in St Peter's. Feast day 22 September.

Formosus *born c. 816, probably in Rome, elected 3 October 891, died Rome 4 April 896.* The son of a certain Leo, in 863 he became bishop of Porto and then engaged in missionary work in Bulgaria, where only the fact that he was already a bishop prevented him becoming archbishop of that country (there was a canonical prohibition technically in force preventing a bishop transferring from one see to another). He served in papacy in various capacities. In 896, however, he was excommunicated by Pope John VIII on charges of conspiracy, and he fled to France. He was readmitted to the church but only as a layman, being restored to his bishopric of Porto in 883, and was one of the consecrators of Pope Stephen V. He became pope despite the legal prohibition against moving sees. During his pontificate he maintained the Roman see's opposition to the patriarch of Constantinople Photios, and twice had to appeal for help against the duke of Spoleto to the German king Arnoul. He crowned Arnoul emperor not long before his own death. After his death his body was exhumed, on the orders of his successor, Stephen VI, and 'tried' for the canonical offence of changing sees. The corpse was found guilty and Formosus' pontificate, including the ordinations he had carried out, declared invalid. The papal garments were then ripped, three fingers of the right hand severed, and the corpse thrown into the strangers' graveyard and thence into the Tiber, from where it was recovered by a monk. Stephen died in August 897 and his second successor, Theodore II, called a synod which reversed all the decisions of the 'synod of the corpse' and had the body of Formosus reinterred in St Peter's, with full honour.

Gaius (Caius) *saint, born Dalmatia (?), elected 17 December 283, died Rome 22 April 296.* The *Liber Pontificalis* describes him as a Dalmatian, and also as a relative of Diocletian, but this must be doubtful. He is said to have insisted on a strict observance of the clerical orders, and assigned deacons to the seven ecclesiastical districts of Rome. He was perhaps imprisoned along with the future popes Sixtus and Dionysius in 257; other accounts associate him with later persecution. The details are decidely confused. Buried in the cemetery of Callistus, his body was transferred to the church of St Caius in 1631 by pope Urban VIII. Feast day 22 April.

Gelasius I *saint, born Rome (?), elected 1 March 492, died 21 November 496.* Possibly of African origin, nothing is known of him, or his family, before his election to the bishopric. He strongly affirmed his position against the caesaro-papist tendencies of the emperors. Within the church Gelasius affirmed the *primatus iurisdictionis* of the bishop of Rome and his supreme authority, even over against decisions of episcopal synods, and insisting on it in his fraught relations with the patriarchate of Constantinople. Further, he argued for the divine origin of the sacerdotal and the political power, claiming their mutual autonomy as well as the greater value of the bishops' sacred authority. In Rome he dealt with Manichaeism and Pelagianism while suppressing the last outbursts of paganism. Buried in St Peter's. Feast day 21 November.

Gelasius II *John of Gaeta, born Gaeta 1060, elected 24 January 1118, died Cluny 28 or 29 January 1119.* The son of John Coniulo, he had studied at, then entered, the monastery of Monte Cassino. He was made a cardinal deacon in 1088, and the following year became chancellor of the Roman church, a post he held for 30 years. After his election to the papacy he was imprisoned by one of the Roman factions, then had to flee the city for his home city of Gaeta, where he was consecrated, because of the advance of the emperor. The emperor set up an antipope (Maurice of Braga, styled Gregory VIII), and though Gelasius was able to return to Rome after the Emperor left, he judged it unsafe, and left for France, where he held a synod at Vienne. He fell ill while there, and went to the monastery at Cluny to die. Buried at Cluny.

Gregory I ('the Great') *saint and doctor of the church, born Rome c. 540, consecrated 3 September 590, died Rome 12 March 604.* Born into a patrician family, he had a legal education and in 572/3 became *praefectus urbis*, a position which allowed him to develop his organizational skills. In 575, however, after the death of his father, he abandoned his secular career and founded a monastery in the family palace on the Celian Hill. In 578 he was ordained deacon and was sent the following year as papal nuntius to Constantinople. He returned to Rome and his monastery in 585, and in 590 became pope. He tried, but failed, to avoid the appointment by writing to the emperor. He came into office as the city was under a plague, and did a great deal to relieve suffering and provide food. To do this efficiently he reorganized the curia and the revenues from the land the Church owned, as well as trying to establish peace in the peninsula. He established good relations with Visigothic Spain, and sent the monk Augustine to evangelize the English. Throughout his pontificate he encouraged the growth of monasticism, converting his family home into a monastery. He was a vigorous upholder of the prerogatives of the bishop of Rome, which meant that the relationship with Constantinople was tense. In 591 he wrote *Pastoral Care,* a reflection on the role of the bishop, which was formative for medieval bishops. His many other theological writings, his homilies and letters and his reform of the liturgy assured him a prominent place in the history of theology and Christian worship. Buried in St Peter's. Feast day 3 September.

Gregory II *saint, born Rome 669, elected 19 May 715, died Rome 11 February 731.* From a wealthy family, he had acted as treasurer in the Lateran while he was a subdeacon, and as deacon had been part of a diplomatic mission to Constantinople (710–11). He possessed considerable political skills, and in 729 persuaded an alliance of Lombards and Byzantines not to lay siege to Rome. He repaired the city walls and restored churches, as well as the abbey of Monte Cassino which the Lombards had devastated. He gave active support to St Boniface in the evangelization of Germany. He rejected emperor Leo III the Isaurian's demand that he approve of his iconoclastic campaign, and rejected iconoclasm as heretical, adding that theology was the business of priests and not of princes. Buried in St Peter's. Feast day 29 January.

Gregory III *saint, of Syrian origin, chosen by acclaim on the day of Gregory II's funeral, consecrated 11 February 731, died Rome 28 November 741.* One of his first acts was to hold a synod in Rome to condemn iconoclasm, which annoyed the emperor, but Gregory also aided the emperor in the struggle against the king of the Lombards in Italy, which restored relations with Constantinople. Gregory strengthened the walls of the city and twice sent embassies to Charles Martell to ask for help from the Franks. Though none came, it established a pattern for the future. Gregory gave his backing to St Boniface's evangelization of Germany, and improved links between Rome and England. Buried in St Peter's. Feast day 10 December.

Gregory IV *consecrated 29 March 828, died Rome 25 January 844.* Cardinal priest of San Marco at his election, he was a firm supporter of papal authority, put to the test when the French clergy objected to his support for Lothair I rather than for Lothair's father Louis I. He accompanied Lothair to France, but had to return to Rome when Louis triumphed. His attempts to mediate in subsequent dynastic struggles were unsuccessful. He consecrated Anskar as bishop of Hamburg, giving him responsibility for missions to Scandinavia. He did a great deal of rebuilding in Rome, and erected a fortress at Ostia to try to contain the threat from the Saracens coming from the south of Italy, where they had been hired by the Lombards as mercenary troops. Buried in St Peter's.

Gregory V *Bruno, son of Duke Otto of Carinthia, born 972, elected 3 May 996, died Rome 18 February 999.* He was a member of the imperial chapel, and accompanied the emperor Otto III in his invasion of Italy. At Ravenna Bruno was presented to the Roman delegation who had come to meet Otto as the new pope: the first German pontiff in history. Although he was at first accepted, opposition in Rome drove him out for a time. He returned with Otto's aid, his authority being established by the brutal suppression of his opponents. Though dependent for his survival on Otto, Gregory was able to display a degree of freedom: but he died suddenly, when still only 27 years old. Buried in St Peter's: his sarcophagus has survived.

Gregory VI *John de Gratiano, born Rome, elected 1 May 1045, deposed 24 December 1046, died, possibly at Cologne, November 1047.* He was a highly principled and respected senior member of the Roman clergy, and provided the funds to persuade the dissolute Benedict IX to abdicate. He was then himself elected. But this transaction seemed rather too obviously simoniacal, even if well-intentioned. At the Synod of Sutri the emperor Henry III declared him deposed and, fearful of his being the centre of an opposition party to the newly appointed Clement II, banished him to Cologne. One of those who followed him into exile was his chaplain, Hildebrand, the future Gregory VII. Gregory VI was buried in St Peter's. *There was an antipope of the same name (1012–13).*

Gregory VII *saint, Hildebrand, born in Sovana, Tuscany, c. 1020, elected 22 April 1073, died Salerno 25 May 1085.* Hildebrand came to Rome when still quite young, and was brought up in the monastery of Santa Maria on the Aventine where his uncle was abbot. He appears to have himself become a monk, possibly in Rome, and certainly spent some time at Cluny: Santa Maria had been a Cluniac house. He was chaplain to Gregory VI and accompanied him into exile, and having thus identified himself clearly with the reform party, returned to Rome in 1049 with the newly appointed Leo IX. He became a deacon, papal treasurer, and prior of the monastery of San Paolo fuori le Mura, and an important figure in papal politics in the reigns of successive popes. He was elected by popular acclaim. He was determined to make the Roman see the effective law-making and law-enforcing authority in western Christendom, and began by a series of synods aimed to improve the moral status of the clergy, particularly opposing simony and clerical marriage, imposing an oath of obedience on bishops and threatening to remove them if they did not impose the papal demands upon their clergy. He also wanted them to make regular visits to Rome to report on their success in carrying out papal policies. He was deeply opposed to the system of lay investiture, according to which monarchs conferred benefices on the senior clergy, thus effectively controlling them – this was incompatible with Gregory's policies. At the Diet of Worms, summoned by the German king Henry IV early in 1076, the bishops attending declared Gregory deposed: Gregory responded by declaring Henry suspended from his royal power – rather as recalcitrant bishops were suspended from the exercise of their office. In 1077, while Gregory was staying at the castle of Canossa, belonging to his supporter the Countess Matilda of Tuscany, Henry asked pardon, which was granted. However, when Henry's rival, Rudolf of Swabia, was chosen as king of Germany, Gregory backed him, after the failure of his efforts to mediate between the two. This proved a costly mistake. Henry defeated Rudolf in battle and then, in 1080, had an antipope elected. In 1083 Henry arrived with his antipope Clement III in Rome, and Gregory had to take refuge in Castel Sant'Angelo. He was freed by the Norman Robert Guiscard, but Robert's troops caused so much havoc in the city that they alienated the people of Rome, and the pope had to flee with Robert to Salerno. Buried in the cathedral at Salerno. Feast day 25 May.

Gregory VIII *Albert de Mora, born Benevento c. 1110, elected 21 October 1187, died Pisa 17 December the same year.* Of a well-to-do Beneventan family, he studied in France and became a canon regular of St Augustine in Laon. He was made a cardinal by Pope Hadrian IV and, after serving as a papal legate on several occasions, he was promoted to be chancellor of the Roman church in

1178. An influential member of the curia, he was elected pope at Ferrara, and was intent on promoting peace in Europe, to prepare the way for a new crusade, when he died suddenly. Buried in Pisa. *There was an antipope of the same name (1118–21).*

Gregory IX *Hugo or Hugolino, born Anagni c. 1160, elected 19 March 1227, died Rome 22 August 1241.* A son of the Count of Segni and a relation of Innocent III, he studied law at Paris and Bologna, was made a cardinal in 1198 by Pope Innocent, and became cardinal bishop of Ostia in 1206. He was a great supporter of the Dominicans and Franciscans, and a personal friend of St Francis himself. His pontificate opened with a clash with the emperor Frederick II, who wished to renege on his undertaking to launch a crusade. Gregory effectively forced him to go, and then undertook a campaign against him in Italy, while the emperor was still in the Holy Land. Frederick returned, seized the papal states and would only release them in 1230 once all ecclesiastical censures he had incurred had been removed. Five years later Frederick accused the pope – wrongly – of having fomented opposition to him in Lombardy. An imperial invasion of Sardinia, a vassal of the papacy, led to Gregory again excommunicating Frederick in 1239, freeing the emperor's subjects from their obedience to him. The emperor invaded Italy and was advancing on Rome when Gregory died. Gregory was extremely active against heresy, creating an inquisition directly under his control, despite the complaints of local bishops, and using the Dominicans in particular in the role of inquisitors. He was a great supporter of the religious orders in general. Buried in St Peter's.

Gregory X *blessed, Teobaldo Visconti, born at Piacenza in 1210, elected 1 September 1271, died Arezzo 10 January 1276.* Elected at Viterbo after a vacancy of three years, Gregory had studied in Paris, and had been a canon of Lyons and archdeacon of Liège before becoming a chaplain to the future king Edward I of England, accompanying him to the Holy Land – where indeed he was when he learnt of his election to the papacy, despite the fact that he was not yet a priest. He returned to Rome, was ordained and consecrated. His pontificate was dominated by his desire for a new crusade, for which he needed, and worked very successfully for, peace in Europe, and for a reunion of the churches of east and west. The crusade was launched at the Second Council of Lyons (1274), which was attended by representatives of the Byzantine emperor Michael VIII Palaeologus, and where a (very temporary) reunion of the eastern and western churches was achieved. At the Council was promulgated the constitution *Ubi periculum*, which was intended to so regulate conclaves that future papal elections would not drag out as long as the one which elected Gregory himself. He died on his way back to Rome. Buried in Arezzo. Feast day 28 January.

Gregory XI *Pierre Roger Rosiers d'Égletons, born near Limoges in 1329, elected 30 December 1370, died Rome 27 March 1378.* His father, William Roger, became count of Beaufort, and was the elder brother of Pope Clement VI. Pierre had been made a cardinal deacon of Santa Maria Nova at the age of 19 by his uncle Clement VI and was then sent to study law at Perugia. He was a pious man, and convinced that his major task after his election was to return the papacy from Avignon to Rome. To do so he needed to re-establish control over the papal states, recruiting mercenaries for this purpose whom he put under the charge of some his own relatives, and of other adventurers such as the English captain John Hawk-wood. His efforts to assert his authority led to conflict with Florence, and a general revolt in the papal states themselves. A peace with Florence was negotiated, and the revolt suppressed. The harshness exercised by one of his commanders at Cesena led to such hostility towards Gregory that, although he managed to return to Rome in September 1377, he had for a time to retire for safety to Anagni. Buried in his former titular church, Santa Maria Nova, in Rome.

Gregory XII *Angelo Correr, born Venice c. 1325, elected 30 November 1406, abdicated 4 July 1415, died Recanati 18 October 1417.* Venetian patrician who had been bishop of Castello and patriarch of Constantinople prior to his election by cardinals of the Roman obedience. A devout man, he was elected unanimously, and took the name Gregory in honour of the pope who had returned the papacy from Avignon to Rome. Although he swore to abdicate if elected and undertook half-hearted nego-tiations with the Avignon antipope Benedict XIII, both were overtaken by events when in 1409 conciliarists at Pisa deposed them, electing first Alexander V and then John XXIII in their place. Gregory finally bowed to pressure from the Council of Constance in 1415 and was made bishop of Porto (and as such next in seniority in the Church to the pope himself) and legate to the March of Ancona for what little remained of his life. Buried in the cathedral of Recanati.

Gregory XIII *Ugo Buoncompagni, born Bologna, 1 Janu-ary 1502, elected 14 May 1572, died Rome 10 April 1585.* The son of Cristoforo, a wealthy merchant, he went to Rome in 1539 after law studies at Bologna, and was ordained. In 1548 he fathered a son, apparently quite deliberately so that he would have an heir to his growing fortune. He was an efficient lawyer and administrator and rose through the ranks of the papal civil service, attending the Council of Trent (1561–3) as an expert in canon law. He became a cardinal in 1565, then papal legate in Spain. It was his success there, and the good relations he had established with Philip II, that led to his election as pope. He was a major figure in propagating the reforms of Trent in the church, especially in improving the standards of the clergy. He opened colleges across Europe, frequently handing them over to the Society of Jesus, whose own Roman College he reconstructed and endowed – it was eventually renamed the Gregorian University in his honour. He also founded colleges in Rome for a number of different nationalities, including the English. His commitment to Catholicism took a more militant turn when he helped to promote the Catholic League against the Huguenots, backed a (failed) invasion of Ireland, and furthered plots against Elizabeth I, as well as encouraging Philip II in the Netherlands, seeing it as a jumping-off location for an invasion of England. The advance of Lutheranism in Germany was halted in his pontificate, and was reversed in Poland, though he had no success in Sweden and talks with Russia collapsed. He was an important patron of missionary activity in the New World and in south-east Asia, especially of that undertaken by the Jesuits, whose headquarters at the Gesù in Rome he completed. He built the Quirinal Palace, and invested a great deal of money in improving Rome for the 1575 Holy Year. His name has been given to the calendar reforms introduced during his pontificate in Catholic lands. Buried in St Peter's.

Gregory XIV *Niccolò Sfrondati, born Somma, near Milan, 11 February 1535, elected 5 December 1590, died Rome 15 October 1591.* A friend in his youth of the future saint

Charles Borromeo, he studied at Perugia, Padua and Pavia, graduating finally in law. In 1560 he became bishop of Cremona, taking part in the third session of the Council of Trent. He became a cardinal in 1583. As pope he proved weak. He was also ill, and depended heavily upon his inefficient and self-seeking nephew Paolo Sfrondati, who became his cardinal secretary of state in 1590. Paolo gave his support to Spanish interests against the French, even sending a subsidy to Paris to win that city's allegiance to the Guise family against Henry of Navarre. Moderate Catholics rallied to Henry, however, hastening his conversion and frustrating papal policy. Otherwise, in the internal affairs of the church, Gregory was active in furthering the reforms, such as episcopal residence, introduced by Trent. Buried in St Peter's though, at his wish, his tomb does not have an effigy.

Gregory XV *Alessandro Ludovisi, born Bologna 9 January 1554, elected 9 February 1621, died 8 July 1623.* He was educated at Rome by the Jesuits (the first pope to be schooled by members of the Society of Jesus), then at the university of Bologna, where he graduated in law in 1575, whereupon he decided to seek ordination. He began a legal career in the papal curia under Pope Gregory XIII, showed himself to be a particularly able negotiator, and was regularly used in diplomatic and important legal positions. In 1612 he became archbishop of Bologna, and a cardinal four years later. As archbishop he was active in improving the training of the clergy. After his election he made significant changes to the procedure for conclaves, forbidding any cardinal to vote for himself, and requiring a two-thirds majority for an election. He also established the Congregation for the Propagation of the Faith (Congregatio de Propaganda Fide), appointing to it some of the most capable prelates available to him, to oversee the missionary work of the church. In Europe he aided the expansion of Catholicism by supporting financially and in other ways Maximilian of Bavaria against his Protestant rival. Buried first in the Quirinal Palace, his remains were later moved to the Jesuit church of San Ignazio.

Gregory XVI *Alberto Capellari, born at Belluno, 18 September 1765, elected 2 February 1831, died 1 June 1846.* He joined a Camaldolese monastery near Venice, taking the name Mauro. After ordination in 1787 he taught, then came to Rome (1795), where he stayed for the rest of his life except when driven out (1807–14) by the Napoleonic occupation. He rose through the ranks of his order, turned down a bishopric, but accepted a cardinal's hat in 1825 – though this was kept secret for a year. He had a strong interest in theology and in 1799 he published *The Triumph of the Holy See*, upholding the independence of the church from all political interference and defending, long before it became an official teaching, the doctrine of papal infallibility. He was faced on his election with a revolt in the papal states, which was brutally crushed with the help of Austrian troops. He demonstrated the same intransigence in his defence of Catholicism. He rejected the overtures of Felicité De Lammenais and, in his encyclical *Mirari vos* (1832), condemned his ideas, rejecting freedom of conscience and of belief, and the freedom of the press as pernicious notions. Such was his belief in obedience to lawfully constituted authority that he denounced the Polish revolt against the tsar in 1831, and in 1844 wrote to the Irish clergy telling them to stay out of politics. On the other hand he also denounced slavery in his brief *In supremo* (1839) and encouraged in mission territories the development of an indigenous clergy. He was, indeed, much devoted to the church's missionary activity, which revived during his pontificate. Buried in St Peter's.

Hadrian I *born Rome, elected 1 February 772, died Rome 26 December 795*. Of a wealthy and powerful family of the city, he was still a deacon when unanimously elected to the papacy. During his turbulent pontificate, Hadrian strove principally to preserve and maintain an appropriate relationship between church and state. At a time when the troops of the Lombard king Desiderius plagued Rome and continually took land from the Church, Hadrian proved himself a successful peacemaker. When Desiderius threatened to march on the city, Hadrian said he would excommunicate the king were he to enter papal territory – the first recorded example of an excommunication being used for political ends. The pope's appeal for help against the Lombards to Charlemagne led eventually to the formation of the Church states, which were to remain in existence until the 1860s. As well as restoring the Roman church, Hadrian also established an agricultural zone effectively surrounding the city. One farm was dedicated to furnishing produce to feed a hundred poor people daily. Hadrian was also very committed to the preservation of orthodoxy. This was demonstrated by his successful handling of Adoptionism is Spain and in the support he lent to Empress Irene in calling the Second Council of Nicea (787), which condemned iconoclasm. Buried in St Peter's.

Hadrian II *born Rome 792, elected 14 December 867, died Rome November or December 872*. Of a prestigious family of which two popes (Stephen IV and Sergius II) had aleady been chosen, Hadrian became cardinal of San Marco in 842. He was chosen to fulfil this office as a compromise between two clerical factions, those in favour of and those against the conservation and implementation of Pope Nicholas I's policies. Hadrian's gentle nature and advancing age meant that he would present few problems to either party. As he strove to enforce Nicholas' policies, papal power diminished and his pontificate was fraught with tensions. He was involved in serious disputes with Anastasius the Librarian, who was involved in the murder of Hadrian's wife and the abduction of his daughter, and in conflicts with several German princes: these remained largely unsolved until his death. Hadrian II received in Rome the Greek missionaries Cyril and Methodius, who had been evangelizing Moravia. They brought with them the supposed relics of St Clement of Rome, traditionally said to have been martyred in the Crimea. Buried in St Peter's.

Hadrian III *saint, born Rome, elected 17 May 884, died San Cesaro sul Panaro, near Modena, some time in August or September 885*. During his 16-month pontificate Hadrian implemented the policies of Pope John III rather than those of his predecessor, Marinus I. An exceptionally severe character, he had an official of the Lateran palace blinded and administered a spectacular punishment to a woman named Maria, having her dragged naked through the city. It was by such measures that he imposed his authority on the opposing factions in Rome. Hadrian met his death – possibly murdered by some of his Roman enemies – while on his way to Germany, where he was to speak to Emperor Charles III (Charles the Fat) regarding a possible successor, Charles having no legitimate heir. He was buried in the Abbey of Nonantola, near Modena, where he was venerated as a saint. His cult was officially approved in 1891 and his feast day is 8 July.

Hadrian IV *Nicola Breakspear, born Abbott's Langley, Herefordshire, England some time between 1110–20, elected 4 December 1154, died Anagni 7 September 1159*. Though information regarding his father is sparse, he is believed to have been a cleric who abandoned his family to enter the monastery of St Albans. Though Hadrian wanted to join him, his father seemingly forbade it. Eventually Hadrian went to France and here he was accepted as a novice in the community of Augustinian canons of St Rufo, near Avignon. He became abbot of his house in 1135. On a trip to Rome, Pope Eugene III urged him to stay on, promoting him to cardinal bishop of Albano (c. 1150). Between 1152 and 1154 he acted as papal envoy to Norway and Sweden and successfully resolved the turbulent ecclesiastical situation there. These achievements led to his swift election on the death of Pope Anastasius IV. His pontificate, however, was fraught with problems. After a cardinal was injured in Rome on Palm Sunday 1155, Hadrian placed the city under an interdict. The potential damage to the economic life of the city, which relied heavily on pilgrims, brought the Romans into line, and Arnold of Brescia, who was the source of the troubles, was expelled. At a meeting between King Frederick Barbarossa and Hadrian on 11 June 1155, Barbarossa reluctantly agreed to recognize, and submit to, the pontiff's supreme authority. As a consequence, Hadrian agreed to crown him emperor. The pope was depending on Barbarossa's support to crush the Normans in the south of Italy, but the emperor returned to Germany. When a rebellion broke out against the Norman leader, William I, Hadrian travelled to Benevento to exploit William's weakness, but found himself instead being besieged in the city, and eventually entering a treaty with William. The treaty gave William control of the south, while William recognized the rights of the papacy over ecclesiastical appointments. Barbarossa regarded the treaty of Benevento as a betrayal by the papacy of the emperor's rights under the earlier treaty of Constance, and once more invaded Italy. He also entered into alliance with

Hadrian's opponents in Rome, forcing the pope to leave the city for Anagni, where he died before being able to carry out his threat to excommunicate the emperor. Buried first in Anagni, the pope's remains were later moved to St Peter's.

Hadrian V *Ottobono Fieschi, born Genoa, Italy, c. 1205, elected 11 July 1276, died Viterbo 18 August the same year.* A nephew of Pope Innocent IV, whom he served as chaplain before being promoted to the rank of cardinal deacon of San Adriano in 1251. He had served successfully as a papal legate. His tactful diplomacy was especially evident on his trip to England in 1265, where he resolved a dispute between King Henry III and his noblemen. After a three-week conclave, Hadrian was elected to the papacy following the death of Innocent V, though he was not at that time an ordained priest. He was still not ordained – and hence not consecrated bishop or crowned pope – when he died at Viterbo, whither he had gone for the sake of his health. Buried in the church of St Francis in Viterbo.

Hadrian VI *Hadrian Florensz Dedal, born Utrecht 2 March 1459, elected 9 January 1522, died Rome 14 September 1523.* The son of a naval carpenter, he was as a young man influenced by the *devotio moderna*. After studying and then teaching theology at the Louvain, he became university chancellor in 1497. A learned and devout man by nature, he was employed by Margaret of Burgundy in 1515 where he was entrusted with the education of the future emperor Charles V. Hadrian was elected after the death of Leo X, at the suggestion of Cardinal Giulio de Medici (the future Clement VII), who proposed him in the mistaken belief that the proposal would be rejected. Hadrian had not foreseen his election, and was in Spain when it took place. He felt ill prepared for it, but after a month's reflection accepted the office as part of God's plan. A foreigner to Rome, his pontificate faced immediate problems not only because Francis I of France and the emperor Charles V were at war, but because he had to try and cope with the Lutheran revolt which his predecessor had all but ignored. Hadrian was the first pope to contemplate and foster reform within the church. Because of this, he faced hostility and misunderstanding on all sides. By the time he faced death, Hadrian was a tired and lonely man who – despite almost single-handed efforts – was unable to bring unity to the church, so leaving it open for attack from the Turks. Buried originally in St Peter's, in 1533 his body was moved to the German church in Rome, Santa Maria dell'Anima.

Hilarius *saint, born Sardinia, elected 19 November 461, died Rome 29 February 468.* The son of Crispinus, he became a deacon under Pope Leo I, who sent him as one of the papal delegates to the 'Robber' Synod at Ephesus in 449, but managed to flee before he was obliged to sign the council's decisions. Some time afterwards he was appointed archdeacon, and given the task of examining the various methods for determining the date of Easter. As pope, he strengthened Rome's hold over the church in Gaul and Spain, and held a number of councils in Rome to settle western disputes. He rebuilt numerous churches in Rome, and constructed the chapel of St John the Evangelist in the baptistery of St John Lateran to commemorate his escape at Ephesus. He rebuked the emperor Anthemius for tolerating the spread of the Macedonian heresy at Rome; he also sent an encyclical to the east endorsing the confessional statements of Nicea (325), Ephesus (431), Chalcedon (451), and Leo's *Tome to Flavian* (449). Buried in the crypt of San Lorenzo fuori le Mura. Feast day 28 February.

Honorius I *born Campania, elected 27 October 625, died Rome 12 October 638.* The son of an honorary consul, he became one of the most controversial of Roman pontiffs because he seems to have embraced a heresy. In response to a letter from Patriarch Sergius of Constantinople, who was seeking to end the debate over the nature of Christ, Honorius wrote that there could be only one will in Christ, a doctrine known as Monothelitism. This was welcomed in the east, and adopted by the emperor Heraclius, but was rejected by later Roman pontiffs as heretical. He showed himself an active, peacemaking bishop in Italy, and encouraged the mission to the English. He took effective control, secular as well as spiritual, of the city of Rome, repaired the aqueducts, built churches, and administered efficiently the papal estates. He was very much in the mould of Pope Gregory I, even to the support he gave to monks: it is not clear that he was one himself, though he turned his family home into a monastery, and brought the monastery of Bobbio directly under the control of the papacy, the first case (in June 628) of what became a common practice, to have members of religious houses independent of their local bishops. Buried in St Peter's.

Honorius II *Lamberto Scannabecchi, born Fiagnano near Imola, elected 21 December 1124, died Rome 13 February 1130.* Scannabecchi was a canon regular, who had served as archdeacon in Bologna then rose to prominence under Paschal II, who made him a cardinal in 1117. He took part in the negotiations for the Synod of Worms of 1122, which effectively settled the investiture contest – or so he believed. Honorius and his supporters wished now to concentrate on reform within the church, a task for which they believed the canons regular were particularly suited: Honorius sanctioned the establishment of the Premonstratensian canons, or

Norbertines, as well as the Knights Templar. In France he brought to an end disputes between Louis VI and the French bishops, and managed to persuade the English king to allow papal legates once again to enter the country. Buried originally in the monastery of St Gregory on the Caelian Hill, where he died, his body was shortly afterwards entombed in the basilica of St John Lateran. *There was an antipope of the same name (1061–64).*

Honorius III *Cencio Savelli, born Rome c. 1160, elected 18 July 1216, died 18 March 1227.* A member of the Roman aristocracy, he had been a canon of Santa Maria Maggiore before becoming a cardinal in 1193. He was an efficient administrator and was credited with improving the finances of the Roman church. He was also tutor to the future emperor Frederick II, whom he crowned in St Peter's in 1220, exacting a promise that he would go on a crusade. Frederick himself, however, was more concerned to consolidate his power in Italy, though he agreed to go on the crusade by the summer of 1227 or be excommunicated. Within the rest of Europe Honorius negotiated peace between rival monarchies to prepare for the crusade. He gave approval to the Franciscan and the Dominican orders, both newly founded, and gave the Dominicans the responsibility of combatting the Albigensian heresy, in the process effectively creating the Inquisition. Buried in Santa Maria Maggiore.

Honorius IV *Giacomo Savelli, born Rome c. 1210, elected 2 April 1285, died Rome 3 April 1287.* His father, Luca Savelli, was a Roman senator, and Giacomo was a grand-nephew of Pope Honorius III. He was created cardinal in 1261 after studying at the University of Paris. He was a popular choice at Rome and although elected at Perugia, where his predecessor Martin IV had died, he returned immediately to Rome and lived there in a palace he had built on family land on the Aventine. He was concerned to try to return Sicily to the House of Anjou – Charles of Anjou had been closely linked with the Savelli family, but Charles' heir renounced the title. He also had little success in establishing better relations with Rudolf of Hapsburg, whom he was expecting to crown as emperor, an event which never happened. In internal church matters he encouraged the newly founded Dominicans and Franciscans, and he also encouraged the study of oriental languages at Paris, in the hope that this might lead to a reunion of the two halves of Christendom. Buried in St Peter's, though his monument was later moved to Santa Maria in Aracoeli.

Hormisdas *saint, born in Frosinone, Italy, elected bishop of Rome 20 July 514, died in Rome 6 August 523.* Possibly of Persian ancestry by his name, but his father Iustus was born in Frosinone, and possibly Hormisdas also. His family was wealthy and he had been married: his son became Pope Silverius I. Before his election he played an important part in the financial affairs of the bishopric of Rome. As bishop, Hormisdas was deeply concerned with the separation of eastern and western churches following the Henoticon of Emperor Zeno, and the demand of Emperor Anastasius that the Council of Chalcedon be repudiated. Hormisdas fought this Mono-physitism by means of a formula of faith which, after the emperor's sudden death in a storm (he seems to have been struck by lightning), all eastern bishops signed (Holy Thursday, 28 March 519): the new emperor, Justin, was himself a supporter of the Chalcedonian formula. Buried in St Peter's.

Hyginus *saint, born Athens (?), elected c. 136 (the year of the death of Pope Telesphorus), died c. 142.* That is the chronology given by Eusebius. However, the *Liber*

Pontificalis claims that he was a philosopher of Athens and reigned for four years and is buried in the Vatican near St Peter. Modern excavations do not uphold this. The Liberian catalogue says that his reign was twelve years long. The *Roman Martyrology* lists him as a martyr, but this is unsupported by other sources. Irenaeus writes that during the reign of Hyginus, the Gnostic fore-runners of Marcion, Valentinus and Cerdo, arrived in Rome. Feast day 11 January, suppressed in 1969.

Innocent I *saint, born Alba, near Rome, elected 21 December 401, died Rome 12 March 417*. The son of a man also called Innocent according to the *Liber Pontificalis*, he was a man of great ability and firm resolution in asserting the powers of the papal office. Innocent succeeded Pope Anastasius I, of whom, Jerome says, he was the son – presumably, as his father was named Innocent, the spiritual son. He insisted on a uniform discipline in the western church based on Roman ways and custom. He endorsed the decision on the Pelagian controversy taken at Carthage in 416, and so informed the fathers of the Numidian Synod, Augustine being one of their number. He tried to defend his friend St John Chrysostom against Theophilus of Alexandria, but could not save him from exile. Feast day 28 July, suppressed in 1969.

Innocent II *Gregorio Paparesci dei Guidoni, born Rome, elected 14 February 1130, died Rome 24 September 1143*. After the death of Pope Honorius II, the chancellor, Aimeric, with a minority of cardinals clandestinely elected Paparesci that same night, and enthroned him at daybreak in the Lateran. The majority of cardinals refused to accept the coup, and elected Pietro Pierleoni as Anacletus II. Innocent could not be consecrated in St Peter's – the ceremony took place in Santa Maria Nova – and had to flee the city soon afterwards, as Roger II of

Sicily backed Anacletus. Both elections were irregular and an eight-year schism resulted, during which the pope travelled in France to win support, then briefly returned to Rome with the help of Lothair whom he crowned emperor in the Lateran, but then had once again to flee the city for Pisa where he set up court. Lothari defeated Roger in battle, and Innocent undertook to follow up this victory by attacking the Sicilian king. He was, however, himself defeated, taken prisoner, and forced into a treaty in which his authority was recognized, but Roger was confirmed in the possession of the territory he had acquired. Politics apart, his reign is significant in that he steered the church once and for all in the direction of the wide-ranging reforms called for by Gregory VII in 1059. Originally buried in the Lateran (in the sarcophagus of the Emperor Hadrian), his remains were later transferred to Santa Maria in Trastevere.

Innocent III *Giovanni Lotario, Conti di Segni, born Gavognano, near Segni, 1160/1, elected 8 January 1198, died Perugia 16 July 1216.* His father Trasimondo was of the Conti family, his mother Claricia was of the noble Scotti family of Rome. He was educated in Rome, and then in Paris – where Stephen Langton, the future archbishop of Canterbury, was a contemporary. He went on for a time to study law at Bologna. Already a canon of St Peter's (though still not ordained), he became a cardinal deacon in 1189. Unanimously elected, while still a deacon, on the day of Pope Celestine III's death, Lotario saw himself as the vicar of Christ (*vicarius Christi*), enjoying the fullness of ecclesiastical power over the church (*plenitudo potestatis*). He used every opportunity to strengthen his political power in the cities and kingdoms which formed the patrimony of St Peter, allying himself first with Otto, whom he crowned as Emperor Otto IV in 1209, then with Otto's adversaries, Philip Augustus of France and the German King Frederick. His great triumph was victory over King John of England, who refused to accept Innocent's nomination of Langton to the see of Canterbury; he imposed an interdict on the kingdom and threatened John with a crusade. The king consented and agreed to hold England and Ireland as fiefs of the holy see, subject to an annual tribute (1213); for years the pope virtually ruled England through his legates. Perhaps his greatest achievement was Lateran Council IV, which in 1215 promulgated a series of pastoral reforms that affected the church for the next three centuries. In 1202 he launched the fourth crusade which, in 1204, led to the capture of Constantinople and the establishment of a Latin empire in the east. He also encouraged the campaign against the Albigensian heretics in Southern France. He gave his support to St Dominic's preaching against the heretics – and hence, implicitly, to the Dominicans (though formal approval came only with Innocent's successor), and to the Franciscans. As pope he issued a number of decretals, which were collected together and published by his chaplain, and he also wrote a number of theological works, though these date from the years before his election. He was buried in the cathedral of San Lorenzo, Perugia, but towards the end of the nineteenth century his remains were brought to the basilica of St John Lateran. *There was an antipope of the same name (1179–80).*

Innocent IV *Sinibaldo Fieschi, born Genoa c. 1190, elected 25 June 1243, died Naples 7 December 1254.* The son of Ugo, Count of Lavagna, he studied at Parma, then at Bologna. By 1223 he was working in the papal curia, eventually heading the papal chancellery and being made cardinal in the late 1230s. Fieschi was elected in the middle of a crisis with Emperor Frederick II at the end of an 18-month vacancy since the death of Celestine IV. He was elected both to reform the church, and to make peace with the emperor; instead, he fled Rome, first for Genoa, and then for France. There he declared Frederick excommunicate and deposed, and did all in his power to undermine his authority in Germany and Italy. While in France he summoned the First Council of Lyons (1245) to tackle church reform, the schism between east and west, and the invasion of Europe by the Tartars in Hungary and the Moors in Sicily. In the end it achieved little, though it was on this occasion that the red hat, as a symbol of cardinatial rank, was instituted. He pushed to an extreme Innocent III's claims to pontifical authority, notably in *Eger cui lenia*, which served to cloak an unlimited personal ambition, and unblushing nepotism. He continued the activity of the Inquisition and, in *Ad extirpanda,* authorized the use of torture. Though Innocent is generally considered to have lowered the prestige of the papacy by his abuse of his power, and his nepotism, he is nonetheless remembered as a canon lawyer of some eminence, and a notable patron of learning. Buried in the cathedral of Naples, which was destroyed before the end of the thirteenth century; his remains were soon afterwards transferred to the new cathedral.

Innocent V *blessed, Pierre de Tarantaise, born Tarantaise c. 1224, elected 21 January 1276, died Rome 22 June the same year.* He entered the Dominican order at Lyon c. 1240, then went to study in Paris in 1255, becoming a doctor of theology in 1259. A Dominican, he held a chair in theology at Paris, and collaborated with Albertus Magnus and Thomas Aquinas in preparing a new programme of studies for his order; a friend of the great Franciscan Bonaventure, he preached his funeral sermon. He was appointed Archbishop of Lyon in 1272, and shortly afterwards was named a cardinal. He attended the Second Council of Lyons and afterwards went on a number of diplomatic missions for Pope Gregory X before preceding him back to Rome at the very end of 1275. On his journey back, however, he heard of Gregory's death at Arezzo, and attended the conclave held there. He succeeded Gregory X on the first ballot, becoming the first Dominican to hold the office of pope. He confirmed Charles of Anjou in his office of imperial vicar of Tuscany. He resumed Gregory's negotiations with Byzantine emperor Michael VIII Palaeologus to implement church union, and demanded that Greek clergy take personal oaths accepting the *filioque,* and primacy of the pope; but he died as the envoys bearing these stiff demands were boarding the ship at Ancona. Buried in St John Lateran. Feast day 22 June.

Innocent VI *Etienne Aubert, born at Mons, Limousin, 1282, elected 18 December 1352, died Avignon 12 September 1362.* The son of Adhemar, he studied law at Toulouse, where he first taught before taking up a post as judge, and eventually joining the the administration of Philip VI of France. He became successively bishop of Noyon then Clermont, and was created cardinal in 1342, becoming grand penitentiary in 1348. He succeeded Clement VI as the fifth Avignon pope. Shaky in health and indecisive, but intent on reform, he was prepared to take tough measures both to reform his own court, and to ensure obedience to the rule in the religious orders. He created fifteen cardinals, of whom all but two were French, and three were nephews. He used the military skill of Cardinal Albornoz to defeat usurpers who had seized the states of the church; the cost of this enterprise caused the failure of a Greek proposal for reunion of the churches, because Innocent could not raise an army to fight the Turks. He had frequently expressed a desire to return to Rome, but death thwarted his plans. Buried in the Carthusian monastery at Villeneuve-les-Avignon.

Innocent VII *Cosimo de' Migliorati, Sulmona, born Sulmona 1336, elected 17 October 1404, died Rome 6 November 1406.* A canon lawyer and an experienced churchman who was collector of papal taxes in England for ten years, before becoming archbishop of Ravenna and two years later of Bologna. He became a cardinal in 1389, and then legate to Tuscany and Lombardy, but made little impact as pope. Fomented by Naples and the Colonnas, there was a popular uprising in Rome after his election, and he had to flee for a time to Viterbo. By 1404 Western Europe had been divided between the 'obediences' of the Roman and Avignonese popes for 26 years. Resolution of the schism was perceived to lie with the French backers of the Avignon antipope Benedict XIII, but civil war convulsed the kingdom. Innocent reorganized the university of Rome, and had Greek added to the curriculum. He created 11 cardinals, three of whom were to become popes. Buried in St Peter's.

Innocent VIII *Giovanni Battista Cibo, born Genoa 1432, elected 29 August 1484, died Rome 25 July 1492.* Son of Arano Cibo, a Roman senator, he spent his youth at the court of Naples and led a dissolute life, fathering two illegitimate children. He studied in Padua and then Rome, and through the patronage of Cardinal Giuliano della Rovere, the future Pope Julius II, he rose through the ranks of the papal curia, becoming a cardinal in 1473. One of the less distinctive popes of the fifteenth century, his election was engineered by della Rovere, nephew of the previous pope, Sixtus IV, who remained the most powerful political operator in Rome throughout Innocent's pontificate. Relations between the papacy and other states featured war with King Ferrante of Naples and the marriage of Innocent's son, Franceschetto, to Lorenzo de' Medici's daughter, Maddalena. As far as cultural patronage was concerned, Innocent was among the less notable of the Renaissance popes. Buried in St Peter's.

Innocent IX *Giovanni Antonio Fachinetti, born Bologna 20 July 1519, elected 29 October 1591, died Rome 30 December the same year.* He studied in Bologna, then entered the service of Cardinal Alessandro Farnese before becoming bishop of Nicastro in 1560. As such Fachinetti participated in the Council of Trent, and became papal nuncio at Venice (1566), where he negotiated the grand alliance that defeated the Turks at Lepanto (1571). He became a cardinal in 1583. He succeeded Gregory XIV, strove to improve the organization of the curia, followed a pro-Spanish policy in France, repressed banditry around Rome, and regulated the course of the Tiber. A scholarly man, he commented on Aristotle's *Politics*, and wrote on other subjects. Buried in St Peter's.

Innocent X *Giovanni Battista Pamfili, born Rome, 7 March 1572, elected 15 September 1644, died Rome 5 January 1655.* The son of Camilo Pampfili and Maria Flaminia del Bufalo, he was descended from two of the most important noble families in Rome. He studied in Rome, and then entered papal service, eventually becoming nuncio in Spain. He became a cardinal 1629. Elected on the death of Pope Urban VIII, despite opposition from France because of his pro-Spanish views, Innocent broke the power of the Barberini, nephews of his predecessor and defended by Cardinal Jules Mazarin. His most significant doctrinal decision had to do with the Jansenist controversy in France, when he condemned, in the bull *Cum occasione*, five propositions taken from the *Augustinius* of Cornelius Jansen, though he failed to stifle the dispute. Despite the entreaties of the missionaries of the Society of Jesus he refused to sanction the form of the liturgy as they had developed it in China – the 'Chinese Rites'. He protested in 1648 against the Treaty of Westphalia because of its principle of religious toleration, on the grounds that this would prevent a Catholic reconquest of Protestant-held territory. Throughout his pontificate Innocent was dominated by his sister-in-law, Olimpia Maidalchini, of insatiable ambition and rapacity, whose influence was baneful and much resented. He made her son Camillo Pampfili his cardinal nephew, but Camillo renounced the rank in order to marry the rich and beautiful Olimpia Aldobrandini. Innocent then promoted a 17-year-old nephew of Olimpia Maidalchni to the cardinalate and, when he proved incompetent, Olimpia's cousin. Olimpia refused to pay the cost of her brother-in-law's burial. Buried St Peter's, but the remains were moved in 1730 to the family church of Sant'Agnese in Agone.

Innocent XI *blessed, Benedetto Odescalchi, born Como 19 May 1611, elected 21 September 1676, died Rome 12 August 1689.* Of an ancient noble family much involved in European politics, he studied first at the Jesuit college in Como, but after the death of his parents moved to Genoa. He began his professional life in the (lay) civil service in Northern Italy, but then moved to Rome and entered the clerical state. His wide experience drew him to the attention of Pope Urban VIII, who made him a cardinal in 1645. He was greatly loved for his piety and generosity while bishop of Novara, a position to which he was appointed in 1650 though still not a priest. Louis XIV of France opposed his election to succeed Clement X, and he had to struggle continuously against the absolutism of Louis in church affairs. For similar reasons, he disapproved of the measures taken by James II of England to restore Roman Catholicism, and especially of the Declaration of Indulgence, which allowed full liberty of worship. A process of canonization, begun by Clement XI in 1714, was long delayed because Innocent had shown favour to the Jansenists, and appeared sympathetic to Quietism. Pope Pius XII announced his beatification (1956) in the altered atmosphere of the twentieth century. His remains lie under the altar of St Sebastian in St Peter's. Feast day 12 August.

Innocent XII *Antonio Pignatelli, born near Spinazzola, Apulia, 13 March 1615, elected 12 July 1691, died Rome 27 September 1700.* Son of Prince Francesco di Minervino, he was sent to Rome to study under the Jesuits and then began a career in the papal diplomatic service. He became a cardinal rather belatedly in 1681, and was then sent to Naples as archbishop. He succeeded Pope Alexander VIII as a compromise candidate, after a conclave of five months. Devoted to the poor, he took firm action to suppress nepotism and to reform religious life. He sought reconciliation with France, and brought about the withdrawal by Louis XIV of the *Declaration of the French Clergy*, which obliged bishops to subscribe to the Four Gallican Articles which limited the pope's authority within France. He put an end to the haggling over the five Jansenists propositions, and in 1696 declared that nothing was further from his intention than to modify the teaching of his predecessor in regard to this heresy. His drawing closer to France was a matter of concern to the other great European powers, but Innocent tried to remain outside the purely political realm, concentrating instead on religious issues – including the reform of the papal curia. He is buried in St Peter's, though his heart was taken to Naples.

Innocent XIII *Michelangelo de' Conti, born in the castle of Poli, near Palestrina, 13 May 1655, elected 8 May 1721, died Rome 7 March 1724.* He studied with the Jesuits in Rome, then entered the papal diplomatic service, becoming a cardinal in 1706. He succeeded Clement XI as a compromise candidate, following the Emperor Charles VI's veto of the early favourite, Cardinal Paolucci, and adopted the name of Innocent III, from whose family he was descended. He endorsed Clement's *Unigenitus* against the Jansenists, and insisted on their submission to his constitution. Innocent took a firm stand in the controversy over Chinese rites, insisting on the Society's obedience. In international affairs he was concerned for economic and cultural development, but constant illness overshadowed his short reign. Buried in St Peter's, though his heart was interred at Mentorella sul Monte Guadagnolo.

John I *saint, born Tuscany, consecrated 13 August 523, died Ravenna 18 May 526.* Senior deacon on his election, and already old, he was pro-eastern in sentiment, and introduced the Alexandrian method of dating Easter to the west. He went to Constantinople on instructions of Theodoric, king of Italy, to dissuade the emperor from persecuting Arians on the Italian peninsula. John was treated with great respect by the emperor, but he refused to grant Theodoric's demand that Arians who had been forced to convert to Catholicism should be free to revert to Arianism. Theodoric was furious and, on the pope's return, insisted that he stay in Ravenna, where he died suddenly, possibly because of ill-treatment. His body was taken to Rome and buried in St Peter's, where miracles were reported. He came to be regarded as a martyr. Feast day 18 May.

John II *Mercurius, born Rome, consecrated 2 January 533, died Rome 8 May 535.* The son of Projectus, he became a priest of San Clemente. He changed his name on his election (the first pope known to have done so) because Mercurius was the name of a pagan god. He managed to maintain good relations with both the king of Italy and with the emperor Justinian in Constantinople. In the continuing controversy over the nature of Christ, John appears to have contradicted Pope Hormisdas when he accepted a dogmatic formulation favoured by Justinian which Hormisdas had rejected. He was perhaps swayed in his decision by Justinian's letter to him which emphasized the supremacy of the Roman see. Buried in St Peter's.

John III *Catelinus, born Rome, consecrated 17 July 561, died Rome 13 July 574.* He was the son of a Roman senator called Anastasius, a Greek name, which may indicate something of his ancestry. Little is known about his pontificate, though much happened in Italy, in particular the drive southwards of the Lombards. John went to Naples to persuade the emperor's representative in Italy, Narses, to return to Rome. This he did, but looted the city and alienated further its inhabitants, already hostile to the Byzantines. John himself, on his return, went to live in the cemetery of Pretextatus on the Appian Way, just outside the city walls. Perhaps as a consequence, he arranged for the better upkeep of the Christian cemeteries of Rome. He also received back into communion the church of Milan. Buried in St Peter's.

John IV *born Dalmatia (his father Venantius was legal advisor to the emperor's representative in Ravenna), consecrated 24 December 640, died Rome 22 October 642.* He was archdeacon of Rome at the time of his election. He held a synod in Rome to condemn Monothelitism – a decision which the emperor Heraclius accepted but the patriarch of Constantinople rejected. Dalmatia was being overrun by Slavs and Avars, and John sent money to pay for the ransom of captives. He wrote to the Irish, criticizing them for holding Easter on the same date as the Jewish Passover. Buried in St Peter's.

John V *born Antioch, elected 23 July 685, died Rome 2 August 686.* A Syrian deacon, whose father Cyriacus may have fled Antioch at the time of the Arab invasions. He had taken a leading part in the Third Council of Constantinople, and was elected unanimously. Politically astute and a learned man, he was, however, ill for most of his pontificate. Buried in St Peter's.

John VI *born Greece, elected 30 October 701, died Rome 11 January 705.* Little is known of his pontificate, except that he saved the life of the imperial representative in Italy, and that during these years the Lombard king came to within a short distance of the city, and John had to spend much money getting him to withdraw, and ransoming his prisoners. It was evidence that the papacy could no longer rely on imperial support to combat its enemies in Italy. As a sign of the papacy's increasing influence in faraway Britain, Wilfrid of York came to Rome during John's pontificate to appeal against being removed – for the third time – from the see of York. His appeal was upheld. Buried in St Peter's.

John VII *born Greece, elected 1 March 705, died Rome 18 October 707.* The son of a Byzantine imperial official, and thought by the Romans to be too subservient to the emperor in Constantinople. Nonetheless he also managed to achieve good relations with the Lombards. Highly gifted, and artistic, he had churches rebuilt and redecorated – though rather in the Byzantine style.

Buried in a chapel of the Virgin, to whom he was greatly devoted, which originally was part of St Peter's basilica, but is now in the grottoes beneath it.

John VIII *born Rome, elected 14 December 872, died 15 December 882.* He was elected at a very troubled time, when there was great need to defend Rome against Saracen invaders. John built walls and established the first papal fleet. He tried, but failed, to form an alliance in southern Italy against the Saracens, and supported Charles the Bald as emperor in the vain hope that he would help to defend Italy. When Carloman demanded the imperial crown after Charles' death, John would not grant it, and was imprisoned in Rome by some of Carloman's supporters – whom John had earlier excommunicated. When he was freed, John went to Provence to find an alternative to Carloman, eventually deciding on Charles the Fat, whom he crowned in 881. John also tried to win the support of Constantinople, the price of which proved to be the recognition of Photius as patriarch. The Council which met in Hagia Sophia in November 879 was manipulated by Photius: John simply agreed to its decisions, adding the rider that he agreed so long as his legates had kept within his instructions, thus achieving the required unity between the Churches. He was the first pope to have been assassinated – he was, it is thought, poisoned and then clubbed to death. Buried in St Peter's.

John IX *born Tivoli, elected January 898, died January 900.* The son of Ramboald, he had been ordained by pope Formosus, and immediately after his election he convened a synod and annulled the sanctions placed on the (dead) Formosus and his supporters. It was also agreed that the election of a pope should be by bishops and clergy of the city alone, though imperial representatives were to attend the consecration. At a subsequent synod at Ravenna these decisions were confirmed, as was the right to appeal to the emperor. It is possible that he was murdered. Buried in St Peter's.

John X *born Tossignano in the Romagna, elected March or April 914, deposed May 928, died 929.* He was ordained deacon at Bologna, and was afterwards archbishop of Ravenna. John was well known in Rome, to which he was a frequent emissary from Ravenna, and was a capable and vigorous leader. It was for these qualities that he was chosen: Rome needed a strong leader against the Saracens. There was, however, a story that he had been called to Rome because he had an affair with Theodora, wife of the powerful senator Theophylact. He did indeed prove to be an energetic leader, constructing an alliance and defeating the Saracens decisively, with the help of Constantinople, in 915. John took part in the battle. He was equally at home in ecclesiastical affairs, and re-established good relations with the patriarch of Constantinople. In Rome itself he was something of a reforming pope, but his attempt to keep independent from the powerful senatorial families led to his incurring the enmity of the Roman nobility, and especially of Marozia, the daughter of Theodora. He was deposed, imprisoned for a year in Castel Sant'Angelo, and then put to death, probably suffocated. Buried in St John Lateran, he was the first pope to be buried within the city walls (St Peter's lay outside them).

John XI *born Rome, elected February or March 931, died Rome December 935 or January 936.* Possibly the illegitimate son of Pope Sergius III – though this is very questionable – he was appointed pope through the influence of his mother Marozia. He strengthened the position of the Cluniacs, but was thrown into prison by his half-brother Alberic, after Alberic had risen against the third marriage of Marozia, imprisoning her, driving her new husband out of the city, and confining John to the Lateran. It is uncertain where he was buried, but despite having been confined to the Lateran during the latter part of his fairly short pontificate, he may nonetheless have been interred in St Peter's.

John XII *Octavian, born Rome c. 937, elected 16 December 955, deposed 4 December 963, died Campagna 14 May 964.* The son of Alberic, who was the virtual ruler of Rome, Octavian was made pope in compliance with his dying father's instructions, and despite his complete lack of interest in religion. He was, however, like his father interested in the reform movements in monasticism. Papal territories in northen Italy were being attacked by Berengarius, the Italian king, so John sought the assistance of Otto I, the German king, offering him the imperial crown. Otto came to Rome, was crowned, guaranteed the papal domains, and told John to improve his dissolute way of life. After Otto had gone John began to make overtures to Berengarius' son. Otto came back, John fled and was deposed. He was able to reinstate himself a few months later in Otto's absence, but fled again on his return. He died, it was said, of a stroke while in bed with a married woman or, according to another version, was strangled by the woman's husband. Buried in St John Lateran.

John XIII *born Rome, elected 1 October 965, died 6 September 972.* The son of John Episcopus (i.e. a bishop), he had been librarian under John XII, then bishop of Narnia in Umbria. He was emperor Otto I's choice for the papacy, and as such was resented by the people of Rome, who were hostile to the ruling nobility. John was first imprisoned, then exiled, but reinstated by Otto, who then supported him. John in return raised Magdeburg to an archbishopric, something Otto wanted. John performed the wedding of a Greek princess to Otto's son (also Otto), in a vain attempt to reunite the two parts of the empire. Buried in Sao Paolo fuori le Mura.

John XIV *Peter Capenova, born in Pavia, elected September 983, died Rome 20 August 984.* Peter was bishop of Pavia from 966, then an official of Otto II's court. He changed his name on election so that there would not be a Pope Peter II. There was in fact no election, he was simply imposed on the Roman people by Otto. Otto, however, died almost immediately, and without his protection John was vulnerable. He was seized by partisans of the antipope Boniface VII, imprisoned in Castel Sant'Angelo and died there, possibly of starvation. Buried in St Peter's.

John XV *born Rome, elected mid-August 985, died March 996.* John, the son of a priest, was cardinal priest at his election by senior members of the papal curia and of the city, apparently erstwhile supporters of the antipope Boniface VIII. He had little political influence but involved himself in the organization of the church in Europe at large, and in 993 became the first pope formally to canonize a saint – Ulrich, bishop of Augsburg. However, he so alienated his clergy, possibly because of his avarice but perhaps because he was attempting to distance himself from those who had backed him at his election, that he had to flee Rome, taking refuge in Sutri. He appealed to the German king Otto III for help, and Otto advanced on Rome, forcing the people who had driven out John to invite him back so as to avoid the wrath of Otto. John had, however, died before Otto reached Rome. Buried in St Peter's.

John XVI *John Philagathos, born Rossano in Calabria, appointed February 997, deposed May 998, died Rome 26 August 1001.* John, a Greek, held various appointments under Otto II, then was tutor to Otto III and archbishop of Piacenza. When it was decided that Otto should have a Byzantine princess as his wife, John went to Constantinople as ambassador. While Pope Gregory V was in exile in Pavia, John went to Rome and was elected pope by the faction opposed to Gregory. Otto, however, gave his support to Gregory, and marched on Rome. Though John fled he was captured, mutilated, degraded from his priestly rank, paraded around the city sitting backwards on a donkey, then shut up in a monastery for the rest of his life.

John XVII *John Sicco, born Rome, elected 16 May 1003, died Rome 6 November the same year.* Little or nothing is known of him, except that he must have been the nominee of one of the powerful Roman families. Burial place uncertain, either Sao Paolo fuori le Mura, or St John Lateran.

John XVIII *John Fasanus, born Rome, elected 25 December 1003, died June or July 1009.* The son of Ursus, a priest, and part of the powerful Crescentii faction – perhaps even a family member – he was cardinal priest of St Peter's at his election, which he probably owed to one of the powerful families of Rome. It seems likely, however, that he wanted to break free of their control by inviting the German king Henry II to the city. He also seems to have re-established friendly relations with Constantinople. He was active in church affairs in both Germany and France, and canonized five Polish martyrs. It is likely that he retired to the monastery Sao Paolo fuori le Mura before his death. Burial place uncertain, either Sao Paolo fuori le Mura, or St John Lateran.

John XIX *Romanus, born Rome, elected 19 April 1024, died Rome 20 October 1032.* The son of Gregory, Count of Tusculum and brother of Pope Benedict VIII, he was still a layman when he became pope. As senator of Rome he had been active in the politics of the city before his election, which he appears to have achieved by bribery. By judicious use of his resources he seems to have consolidated his position in Rome, despite the scandal of being elevated from the rank of layman to bishop in one day. Outside Rome his authority was less obvious. Relations with Constantinople seem to have deteriorated, and although he crowned Conrad II as emperor (in the presence, among others, of England's King Cnut), Conrad frequently overruled his decisions when they affected his dominions. Cnut, however, obtained the waiver of all fees for granting the pallium in return for the annual 'Peter's Pence'. Buried in St Peter's.

John XX through a miscalculation, there was never a John XX.

John XXI *Pedro Julião, born Lisbon c. 1215, elected 8 September 1276, died Viterbo 20 May 1277.* Pedro, the son of a doctor and known in scholarly circles as Peter of Spain, had studied in Paris and taught medicine at Siena. He became dean of Lisbon and archdeacon of Braga, before becoming personal physician to Pope Gregory X, who created him a cardinal. As pope, he made it clear that he was going to continue his scholarly pursuits, which had included a widely used textbook on logic, *Summulae Logicales*, a treatise on the soul, another on the eye, and a manual of popular medicine, *The Poor Man's Treasury*. He retired to his study in the palace at Viterbo, and for the most part left it to others to run the church. He was, however, concerned to broker peace in Europe so that the monarchs might be ready for a crusade, and attempted an agreement with the Tartars to make common cause against the Muslims. The Byzantine emperor Michael Palaeologus, afraid that a further attempt might be made by the Latins to retake Constantinople, made his submission to Rome, along with the patriarch John Beccus, but this had no lasting effect on relations between the two churches. Pope John died of his injuries after the roof of his new study fell upon him. Buried at Viterbo.

John XXII *Jacques Duèse, born Cahors c. 1244, elected 7 August 1316, died Avignon 4 December 1334.* He had studied law at Montpellier, became bishop of Fréjus in 1300, chancellor successively to Charles II of France and Robert of Naples, bishop of Avignon in 1310 and a cardinal in 1312. Although old at his election, over two years after the death of his predecessor Clement V, he was an experienced administrator, and his reform of the papal finances greatly improved its income. He also increased papal control over the appointment of bishops. In 1317 he published the *Extravagantes*, a collection of canon law which became standard. He clashed with the Franciscans, under their minister general Michael of Cesena, over the radical claim that they should own nothing at all because Christ and the apostles owned nothing. This declaration he declared to be heretical. The majority of the Franciscans submitted, but Michael of Cesena and William of Ockham did not, taking refuge with the pope's adversary Louis of Bavaria. In his bull *Quia vir reprobus* the pope declared that the right to own property predated the fall, and therefore was not a consequence of sin. The conflict with Louis was over the succession to the empire, contested by Louis and Frederick the Fair of Austria. Louis, who was also backed by Marsilius of Padua, supported those hostile to

John in Italy, and was excommunicated. Louis then marched on Rome and had himself crowned, installing an antipope. This attempt to browbeat John did not last long, and the antipope submitted to John. John himself, however, ran into theological difficulties over the beatific vision, arguing in a series of sermons that the dead would not enjoy the beatific vision until after the last judgement – a view he to some extent retracted on his own deathbed. John established bishoprics in the Near East and in India, and started the University at Cahors. Buried in the cathedral of Notre-Dame-des-Domes in Avignon.

John XXIII There were two popes with this title:

(a) Baldassare Cossa, born Naples, elected pope of the Pisan obedience 17 May 1410, resigned 29 May 1415, died Florence 22 November 1419. Born into a noble family, Baldassare was a sailor, in effect a pirate, before studying law at Bologna and becoming archdeacon of Bologna and papal treasurer. In 1402 he became a cardinal and was sent as legate to the Romagna and Bologna. His profligacy was legendary, at least before his election during the Great Schism by the cardinals of the Pisan faction (or 'obedience'). He had wide support, both politically and militarily, and conformed to the decisions of the Council of Pisa at least to the extent of calling a reform council to meet in Rome where, given military support, he had been able to establish himself. This Council condemned the writings of John Wickliffe and excommunicated John Hus. The pope's support began to melt away, however. He had to flee from Rome to Florence, and seek the aid of the emperor Sigsmund. Sigsmund wanted a council to decide between the three claimants, and John had to agree to call one at Constance. There all three claimants, the Roman, the Avignon and the Pisan, were called upon to abdicate. John agreed to do so, but then fled the city. He was brought back and, after accusations of gross misconduct and of simony, he resigned.

He was imprisoned in Germany, but released in 1419, when he made his way to Florence, submitted to Martin V who reinstated him as a cardinal, and shortly afterwards died. Buried in the baptistery in Florence.

(b) *blessed, Angelo Giuseppe Roncalli, born Sotto il Monte, near Bergamo, 25 November 1881, elected 28 October 1958, died 3 June 1963.* Born into a peasant family, he attended the village school, the seminary in Bergamo, and the St Apollinare Institute in Rome, where he gained a doctorate in theology in 1904. He became secretary to the reforming bishop Radini Tadeschi of Bergamo, and served in the army in the First World War. His researches in the Ambrosian Library in Milan for his work on St Charles Borromeo brought him into contact with the future pope Pius XI, then the librarian of the Ambrosianum, who sent him, with the title of archbishop, on diplomatic missions to Bulgaria (1924), Turkey and Greece (1934), then France (1944). He became cardinal in 1953, and the same year was made Patriarch of Venice. When elected pope his pontificate was expected to be a stop-gap, but in calling the Second Vatican Council to meet in 1962 he decisively influenced the nature of Roman Catholicism. His major concern throughout his pontificate, and the direction he set for the Council, was pastoral rather than dogmatic. He became personally very popular, and was able to open channels of communication between the Roman Catholic Church and the Soviet bloc, making way for his successor, Pope Paul VI's, 'Ostpolitik'. He promoted dialogue between Catholicism and other Christian denominations, and with the Jews. He was beatified in 2000. Buried in St Peter's. Feast day 3 June.

John Paul I *Albino Luciani, born Canale d'Agordo, near Belluno, 17 October 1912, elected 26 August 1978, died 28*

September the same year. He came from a working-class, socialist, family, and studied in the local seminary, and at Rome's Gregorian University. He was ordained on 7 July 1935, served in his local parish, then in the seminary in Belluno. He became vicar general to the bishop of Belluno, then in 1958 bishop of Vittorio Veneto. A very popular and successful bishop, he became patriarch of Venice in 1969, and a cardinal in 1973. His election to the papacy was intended to mark a turning away from the Vatican's curial establishment and, in holding a press conference and choosing to be invested with his office rather than enthroned as pontiff, this seemed likely, but he died only a month after the conclave. He published, while at Venice, *Ilustrissimi*, letters on topics of the day addressed to characters from fiction. Buried in St Peter's.

John Paul II *Karol Wojtyla, born Wadowice, near Cracow, 18 May 1920, elected 16 October 1978, died Rome 2 April 2005.* The son of a retired officer of the army of the Austro-Hungarian empire, Wojtyla had only completed the first year of his course at the Jagiellonian University in Cracow when Poland was occupied by Germany. Though he had apparently originally thought of becoming an actor, during the war he decided to become a priest. He studied in Cracow and Rome, and after his return to the now-communist Poland, he was briefly a pastor before starting to lecture in ethics at Lublin, and to take another doctorate, in ethics. His interest in the theatre continued, and he wrote plays, as well as poetry and other essays. He was appointed an assistant bishop of Cracow in 1958, archbishop at the very end of 1963, and cardinal on 26 June 1967. He travelled a good deal out of Poland and in 1976 delivered the Lenten retreat to the papal household at the invitation of Pope Paul VI. He was elected in the second conclave of 1978, the first Slav pope, and the first non-Italian since Hadrian VI.

His pontificate was the second longest ever (that of Pius IX being longer by half a dozen years). It was remarkable in many ways. John Paul made 104 journeys outside Italy, travelling 1.1 million kilometres in the process. He brought the reality of the Roman pontiff to multitudes of people, who turned out in their millions to see him. He beatified nearly 1,400 people, and canonized 482 new saints. His first, programmatic, encyclical, *Redemptor hominis*, put Christ as the centre of human dignity. That human dignity for which he campaigned embraced a human rights agenda, which troubled many conservatives, and a commitment to traditional teachings on contraception, abortion and euthanasia, which alienated just as many liberals. On these latter issues the Catholic Church found itself allied to Islamic states. The pontificate was also remarkable for the number of theologians criticized for departing from what the Vatican judged to be Catholic orthodoxy. John Paul did not himself get very much involved in such disputes, but left them to Cardinal Josef Ratzinger (who became Pope Benedict XVI), who served from 1981 as Prefect of the Congregation for the Doctrine of the Faith. The pope became very much a moral arbiter on the world stage. Statesmen attempted to win his approval – denied to them in the two Gulf Wars – and almost all countries who had not already done so thought it wise to enter diplomatic relations with the holy see. The importance of John Paul was demonstrated by the degree of media attention during his long-drawn-out decline in health (it was evident from the early 1990s that he was suffering from Parkinson's Disease, though this was not confirmed by the Vatican until 2003), and by the vast number of dignitaries, civil and ecclesiastical, who attended his funeral.

Julius I *saint, born Rome, elected bishop of Rome 16 February 337, died Rome 12 April 352*. The son of Rusticus, he was elected a couple of months before the death of the emperor Constantine. His successor, Constantine II, allowed Athanasius, exiled to Trier, to return to Alexandria, which led to a renewed outbreak of the Arian controversy, into which Pope Julius was dragged. Julius held a synod in Rome, attended by some 50 western (mostly Italian) bishops, which supported Athanasius. At the end of the synod Julius wrote to the eastern bishops, conveying the decisions of the synod, but also upholding the primacy of the bishopric of Rome (this letter, which is reproduced in Athanasius' *Apologia*, is the oldest papal letter to have survived). The letter, however, pointed out that a decision of synod might be overruled by a council, so Julius managed to have the emperors convene a council in Serdica (Sofia), attended by both western and eastern bishops, though they did not meet jointly. Julius' decision in favour of Athanasius was approved by the westerners, who also laid down the process by which an appeal might be made to the Roman see. The episode shows a glimpse of the very gradually unfolding theory of papal primacy. Buried in the cemetery of Calepodius, although his body was later moved to Santa Maria in Trastevere, which is thought to be the basilica Julii, founded by Pope Julius. Feast day 12 April.

Julius II *Giuliano della Rovere, born in Albissola, near Savona, 5 December 1453, elected 1 November 1503, died Rome 21 February 1513*. He came from an impoverished noble family, but his uncle Francesco della Rovere became Sixtus IV in 1471 and as a result Giuliano was created cardinal, and given many benefices and bishoprics. After helping to secure the election of Innocent VIII, largely through bribery, he began to take a leading role in the affairs of the papacy, but was forced to flee to Charles VIII of France in 1492, when Rodrigo Borgia was elected as Alexander VI. He returned to Rome only after Alexander's death in 1503. After the brief pontificate of Pius III he was himself elected pope. He increased the temporal power of the papacy, removed Cesare Borgia from Italy, brought Perugia and Bologna to submission, and joined the league against Venice. When Venice had been defeated he turned against France, hitherto his principal ally. Louis XII responded by calling a council at Pisa to depose the pope (1511). When the Council, which moved to Milan, declared Julius suspended in 1512, he called a Council at the Lateran and won the emperor Maximilian over to his side. He was a patron of Renaissance art: through his generosity the painting of the Sistine Chapel was commissioned, along with the statue of Moses by Michelangelo in San Pietro in Vincoli (for his tomb), and Raphael's frescoes in the Vatican. He laid the cornerstone of the basilica of St Peter's, the indulgence which brought about Martin Luther's *Ninety-five Theses*. Buried in San Pietro in Vincoli.

Julius III *Giovannni Maria Giammaria Ciocchi del Monte, born Rome 10 September 1487, elected 8 February 1550, died Rome 23 March 1555.* He studied jurisprudence at Perugia and Sienna, and in 1511 was made archbishop of Siponto. He held administrative posts both in Rome and the papal states. Following the sack of Rome in 1527 he was taken hostage by the imperial forces. He opened the Council of Trent in 1545 as papal legate and was its first president. After a somewhat stormy conclave he was elected pope in 1550. He was a great supporter of the Jesuit order and, at first, of church reform, but towards the end of his life lost interest in reform. In 1553, following the death of Edward VI of England, he was responsible for sending Cardinal Reginald Pole to England as legate. He was a patron of Renaissance art, and protector of Michelangelo. Buried in St Peter's.

Lando *born Rome, elected November 913, died February/March 914.* Of Sabian ancestry – his father Tainius was born in Fornovo in Sabina – but otherwise very little is known about him. He is thought to have been one of several early popes created by Theophylact as consul and senator, an office which controlled the temporalities of the papacy. During his brief tenure nothing is recorded of good or evil, and Lando may have been simply a tool of the contemporary Roman aristocracy. Buried in St Peter's.

Leo I ('the Great') *saint, born Rome or possibly Etruria, elected pope 19 September 440, died Rome 10 November 461.* The son of Quintianus, before his election he had already been an influential deacon at the papal court, as his political mission to Gallia on request of the Empress Galla Placidia shows. As bishop of Rome he applied himself to establishing unity within the community by reacting against, for example, both the Priscillianists and Manichaeans. This concern for the purity of faith also guided his actions on the international scene, foremost in the Nestorian controversy. In his *Letter* (or *Tome*) *to Flavian*, the patriarch of Constantinople, he laid down his beliefs concerning the two natures of Christ. But Flavian – with other eastern bishops – was deposed following the Council of Ephesus of 449, as the opponents of the two natures doctrine, the Monophysites, won the day. Leo denounced the Ephesus meeting as a 'Robber Council'. A new emperor, wishing to demonstrate his authority over both parts of the empire, called another council, this time at Chalcedon, which was presided over by Leo's representative. This council accepted the doctrine contained in the *Letter to Flavian*. Meanwhile he asserted the primacy of the Roman bishop, against the claims of the political capital, Constantinople. On the political level he tried to defend his fellow-citizens against the invasions of the Huns, turning back Attila from the gates of the city, though this may have had more to do with pressure elsewhere from imperial forces, and the Vandals, whose king he persuaded to spare the life of the citizens of Rome – though the city was subjected to a fortnight's looting. Of his writings 97 sermons and 143 letters are preserved. Buried in St Peter's. Feast day 10 November.

Leo II *saint, born Sicily, consecrated 17 August 682, died Rome 3 July 683*. Leo succeeded Pope Agatho, and seems to have been elected in June 681, but had to wait some 18 months before receiving the imperial mandate from Constantine necessary for his consecration. The only fact of historical interest with regard to Leo is that he approved of the decision at the Council of Constantinople of 681 to condemn Pope Honorius I as a supporter of the Monothelite heresy. During Leo's pontificate the dependence of the see of Ravenna upon that of Rome was finally settled by imperial edict. Buried in St Peter's. Feast day 3 July.

Leo III *saint, born Rome, elected 26 December 795, died Rome 12 June 816*. A man of relatively humble origins who had risen to be cardinal priest of Santa Sussanna, Leo succeeded Pope Hadrian I, and his pontificate covered the last 18 years of the reign of Charlemagne. Although unanimously elected, he aroused the hostility of Hadrian's relatives, possibly because of his non-noble background, and after a violent physical assault in 799, he fled to Charlemagne's court at Paderborn; escorted back to Rome, he was fully rehabilitated. Shortly after-

wards, on Christmas Day 800, Leo crowned Charlemagne in St Peter's, and the assembled crowd acclaimed
him as emperor of the Romans. Leo accepted the dogmatic correctness of the *filioque*, but judged inopportune
the emperor's request to include it in the Nicene Creed
(810). Assisted by the emperor's rich gifts, Leo did much
to adorn the churches of Rome and other cities of Italy.
After Charlemagne's death in 1814, however, Leo was
once again exposed, and there were plots on his life,
which were put down in a heavy-handed manner, with
numerous executions. Buried in St Peter's. Feast day
12 June.

Leo IV *saint, born Rome, consecrated 10 April 847, died
Rome 17 July 855.* Leo was educated in a Roman
monastery, and rose to be cardinal priest of the church of
Ss Quatro Coronati. He succeeded Sergius II, and his
pontificate was chiefly distinguished by his efforts to
repair the damage done by the Saracens who sacked
Rome three years before. He built and fortified with a
40-foot wall a suburb on the right bank of the Tiber still
known as the Civitas Leonina. Leo consecrated Louis II
as emperor in 850, for the first time renewing the ceremony of Charlemagne's crowning half a century earlier.
In 853 he is said to have 'hallowed' the young Alfred as
future king of England. He sought to bring under his
authority Anastasius Bibliothecarius (Anastasius the
Librarian, later an antipope) and Hincmar of Reims, but
the history of this struggle belongs rather to the reign of
Nicholas I. Buried in St Peter's. Feast day 17 July

Leo V *born Ardea, south of Rome (?), pope from August to
September 903, died Rome early 904.* A parish priest at
Priapi, near Ardea, south of Rome, Leo succeeded
Benedict IV. He was not a member of the Roman
clergy, and it is not clear how he came to be elected.

Possibly it was because, as the clergy and nobility could not agree on a local candidate, they settled for a stranger of whose high repute they had heard from Auxilius, a champion of Pope Formosus. After only 30 days, one of his clergy, Christopher, overthrew him, flung him into prison and installed himself in his place, and then had him strangled. Christopher also died by strangulation early in 904. The location of Leo's tomb is uncertain, but Christopher was buried in St Peter's.

Leo VI *born Rome, elected June 928, died January 929.* A member of the Roman nobility and, at his election, cardinal priest of Santa Susanna, Leo succeeded Pope John X, who had been deposed by Marozia (daughter of Theodora) and her party, and died, probably murdered, in the Castel Sant'Angelo. Nothing is known of his reign, except that he ordered the bishops of Dalmatia to obey their archbishop, John of Spalato (Split, in Croatia), to whom he had granted the pallium, and to be content with their territorial boundaries. He died before his hapless predecessor. Buried in St Peter's.

Leo VII *born Rome, 'elected' 3 January 936, died Rome 13 July 939.* The son of a certain Christopher, he rose through the ranks of the clergy to become cardinal priest of San Sisto. Leo succeeded Pope John XI and owed his elevation to Alberic II, prince of Rome, who ruled the city with absolute control. There is no evidence even of the formality of an election. He appears to have been seriously interested in promoting ecclesiastical and moral reform; he brought Saint Odo, founder of Cluny, to Rome hoping that he would give impetus to a spiritual revival. Leo's surviving letters indicate his interest in Cluny and Subiaco, whose rights he confirmed. He forbade the forced conversion of Jews, but allowed Emperor Frederick to expel them from the cities, unless they accepted the Christian faith. Buried in St Peter's.

Leo VIII *born Rome, elected 4 December 963, deposed February 964, died Rome 1 March 965.* Elected at the insistence of the emperor Otto the Great, by the synod which deposed Pope John XII, Leo, the son of John and a notary like his father, was still a layman. He was put through all the intermediate orders with unseemly haste, and received consecration two days later, this being unacceptable to the people. When in 964 the emperor withdrew from Rome, Leo fled and was deposed by a synod led by John, on whose sudden death, however, the populace chose Benedict V as Leo's successor. Otto returned, laid siege to the city and compelled the acceptance of Leo. A few days later Leo held a synod which deposed and degraded Benedict.

Leo IX *saint, Bruno of Egisheim, born Egisheim, Alsace, 21 June 1002, elected 2 February 1049 died Rome – in St Peter's – 19 April 1054.* The son of Count Hugh of Egisheim, Bruno was educated at Toul where, at the people's insistence, he became bishop. The people of Rome had asked Henry III at Worms to name a successor, and Henry appointed Bruno, who was his cousin. Bruno, however, refused to accept unless he were formally elected by the people of Rome, which was done. His reign marks the beginning of papal reform from its decadence of the past century and a half. He did much to foster a new ideal of the papacy: at the Easter synod of 1049, celibacy was enforced on all clergy; shortly afterward councils promulgated decrees against simony and clerical unchastity. Leo travelled extensively, pressing home the need for renewal, assisted by Hildebrand, the future Pope Gregory VII, Humbert and St Peter Damian. He condemned Berengar of Tours for his eucharistic doctrine that no material change in the elements is needed to explain the eucharistic presence. His later years were marred by military defeat by the Normans at Civitate (1053), as well as a breach with the Patriarch of Constantinople, Michael Cerularius and the eastern church. Buried in St Peter's. Feast day 19 April.

Leo X *Giovanni de' Medicis, born Florence 11 December 1475, elected 11 March 1513, died Rome 1 December 1521.* The son of Lorenzo 'the Magnificent', he received a renaissance education. He was a protonatorary apostolic by eight, and a cardinal at 13 – though this was not made known until he had reached the canonical age of 16. When the Medici were expelled from Florence he went travelling with his brother and with his cousin Guilio, the future Pope Clement VII. He was ignominiously expelled from France, and returned to Rome to live in the Medici residence, the Palazzo Madama, in 1500 until his election to the papacy. Leo succeeded Pope Julius II, and soon disappointed the high hopes that had been placed upon him. He continued the Lateran Council called by Julius, and eventually, in 1516, concluded a concordat with Francis I of France, which firmly established royal influence over the French church. Having squandered the fortune left by Julius, Leo resorted to selling indulgences to finance a projected crusade against the Turks and the construction of St Peter's. This became the occasion of Martin Luther's *Ninety-Five Theses* at Wittenburg, and Leo excommunicated him with the bull *Exsurge Domine* (1520). He bestowed the title 'Defender of the Faith' on Henry VIII of England, in recognition of his book defending the seven sacraments against Luther. Leo and his curia failed to appreciate the significance of the revolution taking place in the Church, and when he died suddenly of malaria, he left Italy in political turmoil, northern

Europe in growing religious disaffection, and the papal treasury deeply in debt. Buried originally in St Peter's, but his remains were moved in 1536 to Santa Maria sopra Minerva.

Leo XI *Alessandro Ottaviano de' Medici, born Florence 2 June 1535, elected 1 April 1605, died 27 April the same year.* A great-nephew of Pope Leo X through his mother Francesca Salviati, Alessandro became a priest under the influence of St Philip Neri. Cosimo I of Tuscany, his second cousin, made him his ambassador to Rome, and he rose through the ecclesiastical hierarchy to become in 1574 archbishop of Florence. Although engaged on diplomatic missions, he took his pastoral duties seriously and appointed men to take charge of his various dioceses, who would apply the reforms of the Council of Trent. He did, however, take up his post in Florence, and was made cardinal in 1583. He succeeded Pope Clement VIII, and adopted his great-uncle's name. He was entirely pro-French in his sympathies, where he had been legate, and persuaded Clement to absolve Henry IV from the excommunication laid upon him. While generally welcomed, the new pope was elderly and in frail health; he caught a chill while taking possession of the Lateran and died before the month was out. Buried in St Peter's.

Leo XII *Annibale della Genga, born Castello della Genga, near Spoleto, 22 August 1760, elected 28 September 1823, died Rome 10 February 1829.* The son of Count Ilario, and a member of one of the noblest families in Umbria, he was destined early for the priesthood. He studied in Rome and entered the papal diplomatic service, in which he was not wholly successful. He was known to have been a great admirer of Pope Pius VI, and of the *ancien regime* that Pius VI symbolized. He was, however, made a cardinal in 1816 and after a brief period as a pastoral bishop (a post he resigned from on grounds of ill-health) and another period in Rome with no post, he rose through the hierarchy to become archpriest of Santa Maria Maggiore and vicar of Rome under Pius VII. Leo owed his election to the votes of the *zelanti*, conservatives who wished to break with the liberal policies of Pius, and with Cardinal Consalvi's political and doctrinal moderation. After his election he moved the papal residence back from the Quirinale to the Vatican. Leo's domestic policy was one of extreme reaction: he condemned the Bible societies, instituted severe ghetto laws that led many Jews to emigrate, hunted down the liberal Carbonari, and the Freemasons; a pervasive system of espionage sapped the foundations of public confidence. His endeavours to restore contact between the papacy and the faithful suffered from a narrow clerical outlook that failed to understand the world developing around him. His death was received by the populace with unconcealed joy. Buried in St Peter's.

Leo XIII *Gioacchino Vincenzo Pecci, born Carpineto Romano 2 March 1810, elected 20 February 1878, died Rome 20 July 1903.* He studied at the Academy for Noble Ecclesiastics, and entered the papal administration, working also as a diplomat. He became Bishop of Perugia in 1842 and a cardinal in 1853, but was not trusted by Pope Pius IX because of his liberal views. Not well known in Rome, he impressed his fellow electors in the conclave of 1878 by his efficiency (he was the camerlengo). He was also thought to be sickly, and not expected to have a pontificate as long as his predecessor. After his election he sought, within the framework of traditional teaching, to bring the Church to terms with the modern age. He continued the policies of Pius against socialism, communism and nihilism (*Quod* *apostolici muneris*), against Freemasonry (*Humanum genus*), and on marriage (*Arcanum illud*). He increased centralization and concentrated religious orders and congregations at Rome. His distinctive contribution was to open a dialogue between the church and society; he directed Catholics to the philosophy of St Thomas Aquinas (*Aterni patris*), and condemned 40 propositions from the works of Antonio Rosmini-Serbati contradicting his doctrine. He fostered study at the Vatican of astronomy and natural sciences, called on Catholic historians to write objectively and in 1883 opened the Vatican archives to all scholars. Leo's most famous manifesto, *Rerum novarum* (1891), upheld private property, the just wage, workers' rights and trade unions; its advocacy of social justice earned him the title 'the workers' pope'. He invited Greeks and Protestants to unite with Rome, but rejected the concept of union as a federation of churches (*Satis cognitum*). He encouraged Anglican aspirations to union, and in 1895 appointed a commission to investigate Anglican ordinations; they were rejected as invalid (*Apostolicae curae*, 1896). Relations remained friendly between the English court and the Vatican; he supported the British government in Ireland, but was disappointed that this did not lead to formal diplomatic relations. A man of deep conservative piety, Leo promoted the spiritual life of the church in many encyclicals dealing with the redemptive work of Christ, the eucharist, devotion to the Virgin Mary and the rosary; he consecrated the whole human race to the sacred heart of Jesus in 1900. He encouraged the work of the missions, especially the formation of a native clergy. Under Leo, the papacy acquired a prestige unknown since the Middle Ages. Buried originally in St Peter's, but in accordance with his wishes his remains were later moved to the basilica of St John Lateran.

Liberius *born Rome, elected 17 May 352, died Rome 24 September 366.* His pontificate was thoroughly coloured by the Arian controversy. He supported Athanasius against the Arian-minded emperor Constantius II but could not prevent Athanasius' condemnation in Arles in 353 and in Milan two years later. Exiled to Thrace, he gave in, subscribed to the Creed of Sirmium and returned to Rome in late 358, where he successfully faced the antipope Felix II. After the death of Constantius he took up again the defence of the Nicene Creed, but to little avail. He built the Basilica Liberiana near the present Santa Maria Maggiore. Buried in San Silvestre, at the cemetery of Priscilla on the Via Salaria.

Linus *saint, a Tuscan, regarded as the first bishop of Rome after the apostles Peter and Paul and conventionally given the dates of c. 68 – c. 78 AD for his pontificate.* Nothing is really known with certainty about Linus. An early Christian by this name sends greetings, possibly from Rome, in 2 Timothy 4:21. St Irenaeus and Eusebius of Caesarea both mention him as bishop. Feast day 23 September, suppressed in 1969.

Lucius I *saint, born Rome, consecrated 26 June 253, died Rome 5 March 254.* Along with his predecessor, Cornelius, he was banished to Civitavecchia by the emperor Gallus, but allowed to return by Gallus' successor, Valerian. He took a liberal approach towards those who lapsed in persecution, despite pressure from the Novatianists. He is the recipient of a warm letter from Cyprian, who salutes him as an honoured confessor. Though honoured as a martyr, he appears to have died a natural death. Buried in the cemetery of Callistus. Feast day 4 March suppressed in 1969.

Lucius II *Gherardo Caccianemici, born Bologna, elected 12 March 1144, died Rome 15 February 1145.* Originally a canon regular of San Frediano in Lucca, he was created cardinal priest at Santa Croce by Pope Callistus II, Caccianemici served frequently as a papal legate of Honorius II, and eventually became chancellor of the papal court. No details of his election as successor to Celestine II are known, but during his pontificate, reactionaries under Giordano Pierleoni, brother of the late antipope Anacletus II, set up a senate independent of the holy see and its rule. To restore his authority in Rome, Lucius took up arms and led an unsuccessful assault on the Capitoline, where the senate was installed, during which he suffered serious injuries, and died shortly afterwards in the monastery of San Gregorio. The cardinals he appointed, including the English theologian Robert Pullen, suggest that he was sympathetic to the reform movement in the church. Buried in St John Lateran.

Lucius III *Ubaldus Allucingoli, born Lucca c. 1110, elected 1 September 1181, died Verona 25 November 1185.* The son of Orlando Allucingoli, he was received into the Cistercian order by St Bernard of Clairvaux, named cardinal deacon of Sant'Adriano in 1138, cardinal priest of Santa Prassede in 1141, and finally cardinal bishop of Ostia and Velletri by Pope Hadrian IV in 1158. Lucius succeeded his patron Pope Alexander III, and resided outside Rome, mostly at Velletri and Anagni. Elderly, honest (one of only two cardinals judged by St Thomas Beckett to be unamenable to bribery), he called a Council at Verona in 1184 which condemned the neo-Manicheans (Cathars), against whom he instituted an episcopal Inquisition. He was concerned to re-establish the papal court in Rome, but succeeded in doing so only for a short period in 1181/2. He maintained good relations with the Norman king of Sicily, but his relations with Frederick Barbarossa were difficult, partly because of the ongoing controversy about the rights of investiture, partly because he refused to crown Frederick's son Henry as a co-emperor. Buried originally in the cathedral at Verona, although his remains are now in the Capitol Library in Verona.

Marcellinus *saint, born Rome, elected 30 June 296, died 24 October 304.* Nothing is known of him before his election, but during the persecution of Diocletian, he apparently complied with orders to offer incense to pagan gods, as did some of his presbyters who later became popes. This apostasy was cited by the Donatists as evidence of his moral failure, and was clearly an embarrassment to later churchmen. According to some traditions, he was filled with remorse for his failing, and days later sought execution at the hands of the authorities. There is in fact no evidence that he was martyred, though he came to be venerated as a saint. His death left the church of Rome without a leader for more than three years, evidence of the severity of the persecution. Buried in the cemetery of Priscilla on the Via Salaria. Feast day 26 April, suppressed in 1969.

Marcellus I *saint, born Rome, elected March 308, died January 309.* Elected only after a difficult succession procedure evident in the long gap of three and a half years between himself and his predecessor. While he was pope he reorganized the city's parishes. With regard to the readmission of the *lapsi* (those who disavowed their faith during Diocletian's persecution), he took a rather firm stance that ultimately led to his removal and exile, probably on the orders of the emperor Maxentius, having first been put to work in the stables of the imperial postal service. He died, still in exile, but his body was brought back to Rome. Buried in the cemetery of Priscilla on the

Via Salaria, but his body was later moved to the church of San Silvestro in Capite. Feast day 16 January.

Marcellus II *Marcello Cervini, born Montepulciano 6 May 1501, elected 9 April 1555, died Rome 1 May the same year.* He studied at Siena and in Rome, was a skilled mathematician and talented in matters of chronology, and was employed by Pope Paul III as tutor to his nephew, which gave him considerable influence on the pope himself. He held a succession of bishoprics, before being appointed cardinal in 1539. He was a committed reformer, and served as one of the presidents of the Council of Trent and on Paul III's reform commission. Much was hoped for from his election: he promptly demonstrated his reforming zeal by forbidding his relatives to come to Rome to benefit from the papacy. He kept his own name on election, but died of a stroke after only three weeks in office. Palestrina's *Missa Papae Marcelli* was written for him. Buried in St Peter's.

Marinus I *(his name was sometimes confused with that of Martin, and listed as Martin II), born Gallese in Tuscany, elected 16 December 882, died 15 May 884.* Marinus was the son of a priest, and had served the papal court from 12 years old, eventually rising to be papal treasurer and bishop of what is now Cerveteri. An expert on eastern affairs, he was used in several crucial diplomatic missions. When elected, he was the first bishop of Rome to be transferred from one diocese to another, contrary to the ancient canons. He was a conciliator, establishing good relations with the emperor, and improving those with Photius, the patriarch of Constantinople. He rehabilitated Formosus, a future pope, reappointing him cardinal bishop of Porto. He also had a high regard for Alfred, king of Wessex. Buried in St Peter's.

Marinus II *(his name was sometimes confused with that of Martin, and listed as Martin III), born Rome, elected 30 October 942, died May 946.* In the mid-tenth century Alberic of Spoleto was in control of both Rome and of papal elections. Marinus, who was cardinal priest of San Ciriaco and about whose earlier life nothing is known, owed his appointment entirely to Alberic and did nothing without his approval. Little of significance is recorded of his papacy. Buried in St Peter's.

Mark *saint, born Rome, elected 18 January 336, died 7 October the same year.* Very little is known of Mark, beyond that fact that he was the son of Priscus, and a Roman. It may have been Mark who laid down that the bishop of Rome should always be consecrated by the bishop of Ostia. He appears to have been a builder of churches, including one on the Via Ardeatina in which he was originally buried, although his remains were later moved to the church of San Marco. Feast day 7 October.

Martin I *saint, born Todi, elected 5 August 649, deposed 17 June 653, died Chersonesus (modern Sebastapol) 16 September 655.* Martin, whose family belonged to the Tuscan aristocracy, had served as apocrisarius, or papal ambassador, in Constantinople. He accepted election without awaiting imperial approval, and immediately held a synod at the Lateran which condemned Monothelitism (the belief that there was only one will in Christ) contrary to the emperor's wishes. The emperor had Martin arrested and, although the pope was very ill, transferred to Constantinople where he was tried and condemned to death. The sentence was commuted to banishment to Chersonesus, in the Crimea, where he soon died, though not before the Romans had elected Eugenius I to succeed him. He is the last pope to be venerated as a martyr. Buried in a church dedicated to the Virgin Mary in Chersonesus which no longer exists. Feast day 13 April.

Martin II see Marinus I

Martin III see Marinus II

Martin IV *Simon de Brie (or Brion), born Mainpincien, France, between 1210 and 1220, elected 22 February 1281, died Perugia 28 March 1285.* He had been canon and treasurer at St Martins, Tours, and then in 1260 chancellor of France under Louis IX . He became cardinal priest of St Celia in 1261 and as papal legate he conducted negotiations for the crown of Sicily with Charles of Anjou and presided over several French synods, including that in Bourges in 1276. He was elected pope – in Viterbo – against his will, and chose the name of Martin in deference to his earlier roles in Tours (there were no Martins II and III, their names being confused with Marinus I and II). He was crowned at Orvieto because of the hostility to a Frenchman of the Roman populace, and mainly lived there. The Romans, to make some sort of relationship with Martin, appointed him a senator for life, a role which he transferred to Charles of Anjou, thus giving Charles overwhelming authority in the peninsula, and in the papal states in particular. Charles' attempt to seize Sicily was frustrated by the rising of the people of the island in 1282 (the 'Sicilian Vespers'), but when the rebels offered to become vassals of the pope, Martin told them to submit to Charles. Instead they offered the crown to Peter of Aragon, who accepted and was excommunicated. Martin also excommunicated emperor Michael Palaeologus, despite his attempts to build friendly relations with Rome, thereby destroying a possible union of Latin and Greek churches. Unpopular with the Roman people, Martin was expelled from

Rome and fled to Perugia. He was a supporter of the Franciscans, whose privileges he extended by the bull *Ad fructus uberes* in 1281. Buried in the cathedral of San Lorenzo, Perugia.

Martin V *Odone Colonna, born Genazzano, near Rome, c. 1368, elected 11 November 1417, died Rome 20 February 1431.* He had studied law in Perugia before serving in the papal curia, being named cardinal deacon in 1405. He was one of the cardinals who went to Pisa to elect Alexander V, and Alexander's successor, Pope John XXIII. At the Council of Constance he at first supported John XXIII, even after he had fled the city, but soon after abandoned him. He was elevated to the papal office by an electoral college drawn from delegates meeting at the Council, though at the time still only in deacon's orders. He subsequently complied with the conciliar decree *Frequens* by calling general councils at Pavia-Siena (1428) and Basel (1431). He entered Rome in September 1420, then set about recovering control of the papal states, which he did successfully, and improved their administration, thus increasing the papacy's wealth, as well as that of his Colonna relatives. He sent embassies to the major European powers, and opened negotiations with Constantinople for the reunion of east and west, though nothing came of this. He attempted to suppress the movement in Bohemia started by Jan Hus, but also without notable success. He abolished the punitive legislation against Jews enacted by Pope Benedict XII, and forbade the baptism of children under 12, unless the baptism was done with the consent of the parents. After his return to Rome he engaged in much renewal work in the city, particularly of the basilicas of St Peter's and St John Lateran. Buried in St John Lateran.

Miltiades *saint, elected 2 July 311, died Rome 10 January 314 (the dates are somewhat uncertain).* Of African ancestry, he was elected bishop of Rome shortly before the Edict of Toleration in 313. Miltiades' role in the legalization of Christianity is not known, but there is no evidence that he had any influence at all. He did, however, play a role in the Donatist controversy. At the initiative of emperor Constantine, he convened a synod in Rome to consider both the election of Caecilian as bishop of Carthage and what the response of the Church should be to those who, like Caecilian, had allegedly apostatized under persecution. At the synod, Miltiades did not endorse the strict stand of the North African bishops and confirmed the election of Caecilian, excommunicating his rival Donatus. It was Miltiades who ordered the practice of distributing a piece of the consecrated eucharistic bread (the *fermentum*) to all the churches of Rome. Buried in the cemetery of St Callistus on the Appian Way, although his remains may later have been moved to San Silvestro in Capite. Feast day 10 December.

Nicholas I *saint, born Rome 820, elected pope on 24 April 858, died Rome 13 November 867.* Made subdeacon by Pope Sergius II and deacon by Leo IV, he was chosen to succeed Pope Benedict III by the emperor Louis II. In the difficulties after the collapse of Charlemagne's empire, he upheld Christian morality and authority against ambitious princes and worldly bishops. Despite the acquiescence of the archbishops of Trier and Cologne in the desire of Lothair II to divorce his wife in order to marry his mistress, Nicholas refused to grant the request, even when Lothair's brother invaded Rome, forcing Nicholas to take refuge in St Peter's. He asserted his authority over the bishops of the western church, and tried to do similarly in the east, clashing with the Patriarch Photius of Constantinople, whose appointment he considered uncanonical. Photius excommunicated the pope in 867, but Nicholas replied that the see of Rome was not subject to any other court. He built and endowed several churches in Rome. He encouraged the church's missionary activity and secured the position of the papacy in western Europe. Buried in St Peter's. Feast day 13 November.

Nicholas II *Gerard, born Lorraine or Burgundy, elected pope 6 (?) December 1058, died Florence 19 or 27 July 1061.* A canon of Liège, he became bishop of Florence in 1046 and was chosen as pope by the reform party among the cardinals, with the backing of the imperial court. However, the Roman nobility had already elected John of Velletri, who took the title Benedict X, and it was only with military support that Nicholas was able to enter Rome, where he and his reformist party could only slowly take charge of the church. Benedict was deposed and banished by the imperial authorities. At Easter 1059 Nicholas held a synod in the Lateran to remove papal elections from factional and imperial influence. It was decided that only cardinal bishops should have a vote, but their choice was to be confirmed by the other cardinals, and then by the people of Rome. The synod also condemned clerical simony and concubinage.

Nicholas III *Giovanni Gaetano Orsini, born Rome, c. 1215, elected 25 November 1277, died Soriano, near Viterbo, 22 August 1280.* The son of Matteo (Rosso) Orisini, and through his mother related to the dukes of Gaeta, he came from a very powerful lineage. He was made cardinal deacon of St Nicola in Carcere in 1244, and became grand inquisitor and protector of the Franciscans. He rose to be rector of Santa Sabina and, through the appointment of other relatives and friends to the cardinalate, an extremely influential member of the college of cardinals. He played a major role in the election of Pope John XXI, who made him archpriest of St Peter's. Elected in Viterbo, he was chiefly concerned during his pontificate to ensure the independence of the papacy by restricting the role of other major players on the Italian peninsula, particularly Charles of Anjou, king of Sicily but also a Roman senator. He managed to define the boundaries of the papal states until they were over-run in the nineteenth-century unification of Italy. In order to prevent disputes over this territory, he arranged an alliance between the Habsburg and Anjou families. The negotiations to this end had not been completed at his death. He improved the efficiency of the papal curia, restored St Peter's, and made the Vatican Palace beside St Peter's his normal place of residence – the first pope to do so. He also entered into negotiations with the Byzantine emperor, Michael Palaeologus, for a possible reunion of the churches, and prevented an attack on Constantinople by Charles of Sicily. Buried in St Peter's, though he died in Viterbo.

Nicholas IV *Girolamo Maschi, born Liciano, near Ascoli, March of Ancona, 3 September 1227, elected 15 then 22 February 1288, died Rome 4 April 1292.* At an early age he entered the Franciscan order, and became provincial of Dalmatia and then general of the order, in succession to St Bonaventure. In 1278, while on a mission to promote peace between France and Castile, he was made a cardinal priest and in 1281 cardinal bishop of Palestrina. In 1287 a divided conclave met to elect a pope, but an outbreak of fever decimated the electors, all except Maschi fleeing Rome. They met again on 15 February 1288 and unanimously chose Nicholas after a vacancy of almost 11 months, but a second election was required to overcome his reluctance. He was the first Franciscan pope, and used the Franciscans as missionaries to the east, where he hoped to gain converts as a bulwark against the armies of Islam: Acre, the last stronghold of the Christians in the Holy Land, fell during his pontificate. In Italy he supported the Angevins against the Aragonese in the struggle for the kingdom of Sicily. He built a papal residence near Santa Maria Maggiore, and restored that basilica as well as the basilica of St John Lateran. Buried in Santa Maria Maggiore.

Nicholas V *Tommaso Parentucelli, born Sarzana 15 November 1397, elected 6 March 1447, died Rome 25 March 1455.* A humanist scholar of modest origins (he was the son of a doctor, Bartolomeo), Parentucelli had little money and worked as a tutor in Florence before returning to the University of Bologna to study theology. He entered the service of the bishop of Bologna, and accompanied the bishop to Rome, when he was made a cardinal. He in turn became bishop of Bologna and a cardinal (in December 1446), being used by the pope as a successful diplomat. He had therefore been a cardinal for only a matter of months before being elected to the papal office. His pontificate witnessed the end of the schismatic threat from the Council of Basel and the fall of Constantinople to the Ottoman Turks (1453). The New Learning was supported by the pope's own literary activities, his foundation of the Vatican Library and his patronage of Italian humanists and Greek scholars, including Bessarion. His ambitious urban planning in Rome initiated, among other projects, the rebuilding of St Peter's basilica, funding for which came from the Jubilee of 1450. In 1452 he crowned Frederick III as emperor, the last such coronation to take place, and one in which papal authority was more on display than was imperial power. He attempted both to remain neutral and to keep the peace in Italy, in great part to enable a more united front against the Turks. Buried in St Peter's. *There was an antipope of the same name (1328–30).*

Paschal I *saint, born Rome, elected 25 January 817, died Rome 17 May 824.* He studied in the school attached to the Lateran, joined the papal civil service and, when elected, was abbot of the monastery of St Stephen. Relations between pope and emperor (Louis the Pious) were good, until Louis' son Lothair came to Rome to be crowned co-emperor (for the second time) in 823. Lothair, however, appeared to usurp some papal author-ity while in the city, something welcomed by Paschal's enemies. Two of them were executed, much to the anger of Louis, though Paschal denied responsibility. Paschal protested against the revival of iconoclasm in the east, and provided refuge for Greek monks driven out by the iconoclasts. He built several splendidly decorated churches, but was, however, unpopular in Rome itself, especially among the nobility, for his dictatorial manner. An unruly crowd interrupted his funeral, and his burial place is uncertain, though the *Liber Pontificalis* claims it was St Peter's. Feast day 14 May, suppressed in 1969.

Paschal II *Rainerius, born at Bieda di Galatea, in the Romagna, elected 13 August 1099, died Rome 21 January 1118.* Paschal entered a monastery as a boy – it is unclear where – and was eventually sent to Rome by his abbot on business for the abbey. He stayed and was appointed abbot of San Lorenzo fuori le Mura, and then became cardinal priest of San Clemente under Pope Gregory VII. He served as legate in Spain under Pope Urban II. He succeeded Urban – the election took place in San Clemente – and renewed the papal decrees against lay investiture, in 1102 excommunicating King Henry IV of Germany. In August 1110, Henry V marched on Rome, determined to obtain imperial coronation and the right of investiture. A compromise was reached in Sutri in February 1111 by which Henry renounced investiture (bestowal of ring and crozier), the church agreed to forego the *regalia*, and bishops and abbots were to retain tithes and other offerings. The agreements were repudiated by both sides during the coronation ceremony in St Peter's, and Henry had Paschal and his cardinals arrested and held for two months until Paschal agreed to grant the right of investiture to emperors. The coronation then went ahead. Paschal, accused by opponents of lay investiture of heresy, considered abdicating, and finally condemned it again in 1116. When Henry decided to come to Rome again in 1117 Paschal left the city, but returned again just before his death in Castel San'Angelo. Buried in St John Lateran.

Paul I *saint, born Rome, elected 29 May 757, died Rome 28 June 767.* Paul succeeded his brother Pope Stephen II, and his pontificate is chiefly remembered for his close alliance with Pepin III of the Franks. He reorganized the temporal power of the papacy and, fearing an invasion by the Byzantines, tried unsuccessfully to effect a reconciliation with the iconoclastic emperor of the east, Constantine Copronymus. He turned his family home into a monastery, San Silvestro in Capite, and moved the bodies of three pope saints there. He died at San Paolo fuori le Mura, where he was first buried, though his remains were moved a few months later to St Peter's. Feast day 28 June.

Paul II *Pietro Barbo, born Venice 23 February 1417, elected 30 August 1464, died Rome 26 July 1471.* A Venetian patrician who belonged to an extensive clerical dynasty and whose early career was determined by the patronage of his uncle Pope Eugenius IV. He became cardinal deacon of Santa Maria Nova in 1440, and then later of

San Marco. A popular figure because of his generosity, he was chosen as pope on the first ballot. He continued the work of previous fifteenth-century popes in attempting to impose central authority on the papal states. He set about reforming the curia, abolished the college of abbreviators (1466), and suffered being called an illiterate persecutor of learning for having suppressed in 1468 the Roman academy on religious grounds. He was, however, friendly to Christian scholars. He began negotiations with Ivan III for the union of the Russian church with the Roman see; he carried on fruitless negotiations (1469) with Emperor Frederick III for a crusade against the Turks. Though not a man for radical reforms or unusual views, Paul had an attractive personality. Much of his wealth went into building the Palazzo di St Marco (now Palazzo Venezia), where he chose to live and where he housed his collection of antiquities and objet d'art. Buried in St Peter's.

Paul III *Alessandro Farnese, born Camino 29 February 1468, elected 13 October 1534, died Rome 10 November 1549.* A cardinal, of St Cosma e Damiano, at 26, and given to a life of luxury in the circle of Cosmo de Medici, he owed his rise to his sister Giulia, who was the mistress for a time of Pope Alexander VI. Farnese himself, before his conversion to a more spiritual life around 1513, produced a number of children – and made two of his grandchildren cardinals shortly after his election. There were numerous other examples of nepotism – he made his son, Pierluigi, Duke of Parma and Piacenza, and advanced others of his family. He was a patron of the Catholic reform: he appointed as cardinals men of virtue and scholarship, favoured the new orders such as the Ursulines or the Barnabites, and approved the Society of Jesus in 1540. In 1542 he restored the Inquisition, but procrastinated in the matter of a reform council, though this finally opened at Trent in 1545, having been announced three years before. Less successful in political matters, he brokered a truce to permit a united front against the Turks, though the alliance did not long survive, and failed to get Protestant support, or to halt the Turkish advance further into Europe. He further alienated England with his bull against Henry VIII in 1538, and had no success in checking the spread of Protestantism. A lover and patron of art and scholarship, he commissioned Michelangelo to paint the *Last Judgement*, and to resume work on St Peter's. Buried in St Peter's.

Paul IV *Gian Pietro Carafa, born Capriglio, near Avellino, 28 June 1476, elected 23 May 1555, died Rome 18 August 1559.* He came from a prominent Neapolitan family, and owed his rise to his uncle, a cardinal, who gave up his own diocese of Chieti in favour of his nephew. A member of the circle of reform cardinals favoured by Pope Paul III, Carafa founded, with St Cajetan, the Theatine Order in 1524 (it took its name from the Latin for Chieti), aimed at reform of the Church from its grave abuses and scandals, and himself became a member. He advised Pope Paul III to establish the Roman Inquisition, and was a member of the Inquisition from its inception. As pope he was ineffectively active in the suppression of heresy, and produced in 1559 the first papal *Index of Forbidden Books*, which earned him great unpopularity: the *Index* was moderated on his death. A severe and reforming pope, he mistrusted the Council of Trent, which he would not allow to reopen. Hostile to Spanish domination of the kingdom of Naples, he had to sue for peace after the defeat of his nephew Carlo Carafa and the invasion of the papal states by the Duke of Alba. The Romans rioted when he died, displaying relief that his harsh rule had ended. Buried first in St Peter's, his remains were later moved to a tomb in Santa Maria sopra Minerva.

Paul V *Camillo Borghese, born Rome 17 September 1552 elected 16 May 1605, died Rome 28 January 1621.* Borghese studied law at Perugia and Padua, joined the papal curia, taking his father Marcantonio's place as a lawyer of the consistory, and rose through its ranks to become cardinal in 1596 (on his appointment as ambassador to King Philip of Spain), and Inquisitor in 1603. He remained neutral in the conflict between Spain and France, which contributed to his election in succession to Pope Leo XI. Like so many of his predecessors he promoted his relatives, but in practice retained authority for himself. He provoked disputes with the Italian states over ecclesiastical rights; others yielded, but Venice resisted, determined to be supreme in its own territory, despite excommunication and interdict. Paul condemned the oath that James I of England demanded of Catholics following the Gunpowder Plot. He censured Galileo Galilei (1616) for teaching the Copernican theory of the solar system, and suspended Copernicus' treatise 'until corrected'. He approved the Congregation of the Oratory, the French Oratory of Pierre de Bérulle; he canonized Charles Borromeo and Frances of Rome, and beatified Ignatius Loyola, Francis Xavier, Philip Neri and Teresa of Avila. He completed St Peter's and extended the Vatican Library, moving the papal archives into the Vatican. He engaged in a number of building projects, and constructed the 'Pauline' chapel in Santa Maria Maggiore, where he is buried.

Paul VI *Giovanni Battista Montini, born Concesio, Lombardy, 26 September 1897, elected 21 June 1963, died Castel Gandolfo, 6 August 1978.* His father had been a politician, and Montini displayed a keen interest in

Italian politics. He was ordained in 1920, went to Rome to study, then joined the secretariat of state. While in the secretariat he served also as chaplain to Catholic students, by which means becoming friendly with many who would become prominent in the post-war years, including Aldo Moro, murdered during Montini's pontificate. His liberal sympathies were an irritation to Mussolini. He was appointed Archbishop of Milan in 1954, and a cardinal four years later. Montini succeeded Pope John XXIII, having played a major role in preparing Vatican Council II (1962–5). His attitude to the first session, at which he spoke only twice, was cool, not to say critical. However, following his election, Paul opened the second session in September 1963, and promulgated its decrees. A progressive in social and political matters, and very much aware of the developing world, Paul issued *Progressio populorum* (1967), a call for social justice in the evolution of developing lands, visited South America, Africa, India, and the Holy Land, and pleaded for peace at the UN General Assembly in 1965. His ecumenical gestures included reconciliation with orthodox patriarch Athenagoras in Istanbul, and meeting Michael Ramsay, archbishop of Canterbury, with whom he established the Anglican-Roman Catholic International Commission; he also met heads of the Armenian and Jacobite churches and of the World Council of Churches. Despite his reform of the curia, which diminished Italian influence and reduced the pomp and circumstance of the papacy, in theology Paul was a conservative: his encyclicals, *Mysterium fidei*, reasserted traditional eucharistic doctrine, while paving the way for liturgical reform; *Humanae vitae* condemned artificial methods of birth control; and *Sacerdotalis coelibatus* insisted on the necessity of priestly celibacy in the Latin rite, and also approved the 1977 declaration by the Congregation for the Doctrine of the Faith against the ordination of women to the priesthood. He was very well read, and numbered scholars such as Maritain among his friends. Buried in St Peter's.

Pelagius I *born Rome, consecrated 16 April 556, died 3 March 561.* He was a deacon and went with Pope Agapitus I to Constantinople, and succeeded Vigilius as *apocrisiarius,* or papal ambassador, in 537. He had been opposed to the condemnation, by the emperor Justinian, of the Antiochenes, Theodore of Mopsuestia, Theodoret of Cyrrus and Ibas of Edessa (the 'Three Chapters' controversy), and wrote eloquently against it. He had a change of heart later, however, when it became clear that the emperor wished to appoint him as pope in succession to Vigilius, who died in exile in June 555. He was unwelcome in Rome, and after several months he still could not find three bishops to officiate at his consecration, the ceremony had eventually to be performed with two bishops and a presbyter representing the bishop of Ostia. He sought to establish his orthodoxy with both Church and political leaders, and set about restoring the physical, social and political structures of Rome after the devastation caused by the Gothic wars. He reorganized papal finances, relieved the situation of those reduced to poverty and generally began to bring Rome back to a feeling of normality. In so doing he won over many of his earlier opponents, but not the northern Italian bishops, who were not to be in communion with Rome again for another century and a half. Buried in St Peter's.

Pelagius II *born Rome, elected August 579, died Rome (of the plague) 7 February 590.* The son of a certain Unigild (which suggests that his ancestry was German), he tried to gain the assistance of both Constantinople and the Frankish king against the Lombard threat, but secured the support of neither. He eventually negotiated a truce with the Lombards, though only for a few years. He continued rebuilding the physical and social fabric in Rome, turned his family house into an almshouse, and was probably responsible for moving the high altar in St Peter's to the position immediately above the relics of the saint. He tried, without success, to heal the breaches with the northern Italian bishops caused by the 'Three Chapters' controversy, and came into dispute with the patriarch of Constantinople over the meaning and use by the latter of the term 'ecumenical patriarch', which appeared to suggest primacy. He sent the deacon Gregory, later Pope Gregory the Great, to Constantinople as his *apocrisarius*, or ambassador. Buried in St Peter's.

Peter *saint, Simon, born Bethsaida in Galilee, came to Rome c. 60, died Rome c. 67.* His father's name, Jonah, suggests a Hebrew origin: the names of his brothers Andrew and Philip indicate Greek influence. He worked as a fisherman before being called by Jesus to be an apostle, and to be leader of the apostles: 'You are Peter, and upon this rock I will build my church' (Matthew 16:17–18). The title *princeps*, usually translated as 'prince' (of the apostles), was given to Peter in the fourth century: he was the *princeps* of the church, as the emperor was of the empire. Little is known of his apostolate, though the Acts of the Apostles attributes to him the first conversion of a pagan to Christianity. Nonetheless, Peter appears to have originally believed that such converts should conform to Jewish practices. On this he was challenged by St Paul, the issue being decided in Paul's favour at a gathering, or council, of the apostles in Jerusalem. Early Christian chroniclers attributed to him the foundation of the church at Antioch whence, it seems, he came to Rome, where there was already a Christian community. He was martyred in the persecution of Nero. The fact that he was ever in Rome, questioned by Martin Luther and by many others since, is now generally accepted. Papal authority depends upon the commission by Jesus to Peter, the bishops of Rome being, according to tradition, in direct descent from the apostle. To call Peter 'bishop of Rome' is, however, an anachronism: the notion of a single individual presiding over the local Christian community, and especially over its liturgy, had not emerged in Peter's lifetime – nor, indeed, during the lifetime of his immediate 'successors'. Buried on the Vatican hill: St Peter's basilica is almost certainly over the site of his tomb. Feast day (with St Paul) 29 June.

Pius I *saint, born Aquileia, elected c. 142, died Rome c. 155.* Both Eusebius and St Jerome place his accession in the fifth year of Antonius Pius (142), and his reign as 15 years. He was, according to the *Muratorian Fragment*, a brother of Hermas, author of the *Shepherd,* an account of a series of revelations made to Hermas by different heavenly visitors. It was Pius who condemned the heretic Marcion. There is no evidence for the tradition that Pius died a martyr. Feast day 11 July.

Pius II *Enea Silvio Piccolomini, born Corsignano (subsequently Pienza), near Siena, 18 October 1405, elected 27 August 1458, died Ancona 14 August 1464.* From a leading Sienese family, Piccolomini was a prolific writer of history, poetry, biography and autobiography. He began his career as secretary to a series of distinguished prelates, then became a secretary of the Council of Basle. Though he at first opposed Pope Eugenius IV, he subsequently negotiated the return of Germany to Eugenius' obedience (1445), was ordained priest in 1446, became bishop of Trieste, and Siena (1449), and cardinal of Santa Sabina (1456), serving in the latter role as advisor to Pope Callistus III on German affairs. Upon election to the papacy, he rejected the worldliness of his previous life and championed the cause of papal primacy, a particular triumph being the 1462 revocation of the Pragmatic Sanction of Bourges. Pius called the Congress of Mantua (1459) to co-ordinate a crusade against the Ottomans, and died at Ancona after vainly waiting for military support from the Christian powers. Originally buried in St Peter's, his tomb in 1614 was moved to the church of San Andrea della Valle.

Pius III *Francesco Todeschini-Piccolomini, born Siena 9 May 1439, elected 22 September 1503, died Rome 18 October the same year.* He was appointed archbishop of Siena, aged 22, by his uncle Pius II, who also created him cardinal deacon of San Eustachio, and finally vicar of Rome when Pius II went off to Ancona to await the start of the (abortive) crusade. He lived outside Rome after the death of his uncle, but he was appointed legate by Pope Sixtus IV to the Diet of Regensburg, and Sixtus also asked him to secure the restoration of ecclesiastical authority in Umbria. He opposed the policy of Pope Alexander VI, and was elected pope amid the upheavals following the death of the latter, through the interested influence of Cardinal della Rovere, afterwards Pope Julius II. He permitted Cesare Borgia to return to Rome, and took in hand the reform of the curia. He was unusual among popes of the age for not practising nepotism. A man of blameless life, he was also a patron of the arts. Buried originally in St Peter's, his remains were moved in 1614 to the church of San Andrea della Valle.

Pius IV *Gian Angelo de' Medici, born Milan 31 March 1499, elected 26 December 1559, died Rome 9 December 1565.* Not related to the Florentine Medicis, he grew up in somewhat straitened circumstances. He entered the service of the papal curia and held several offices, eventually becoming archbishop of Ragusa in 1545, at which point he took orders. He was made cardinal by Paul III, and papal legate in Romagna by Julius III. After a fraught conclave, he succeeded Paul IV, reversed his imperial policy and brought his Carafa relatives to trial; Pius' own nepotism had a happy result for the church in the cardinalate of his nephew, Saint Charles Borromeo. His greatest achievement is the Council of Trent, which he successfully concluded (1563), and whose decrees he executed, namely: a new *Index of Forbidden Books*; the *Catechism of the Council of Trent* or Roman Catechism; the imposition of the Professio Fidei Tridentina (Tridentine Profession of Faith) on all holders of ecclesiastical office; and reformation of the College of Cardinals. He tried to insist on Trent's requirement of residence for all bishops, and founded the Roman College – which eventually became the Gregorian University – to be run by the Society of Jesus. Originally buried in St Peter's, his remains were moved in 1583 to Santa Maria degli Angeli.

Pius V *saint, Michele Ghislieri, born Boscomarengo, Lombardy, 17 January 1504, elected 7 January 1566, died Rome 1 May 1572.* From a peasant family, he was educated by the Dominicans, and then entered the order aged 14. He was ordained in 1528 and had an academic career before entering the holy office as an inquisitor (c. 1546), eventually becoming cardinal in 1557 and grand inquisitor the following year. During the pontificate of Pius IV he was out of favour, and turned his attentions instead to running his diocese. Charles Borromeo assisted him in being elected as Pius IV's successor. He worked zealously for the reform of the church and compelled bishops and clergy to accept the recommendations of the Council of Trent. He struggled against the spread of the Reformation, in France supporting war against the Huguenots with financial aid, encouraging the Spanish invasion of England, and famously and disastrously excommunicating Elizabeth I (1570), when she imprisoned Mary Stuart. He succeeded in forming the alliance of Spain and Venice, which defeated the Ottoman Turks at Lepanto in 1571. In Rome he expelled prostitutes and closed down brothels, and made Jews live in ghettoes in an effort to make them convert. He imposed a Rome-approved liturgy throughout the church, overriding local diocesan variants (and those used by religious orders) unless they were at least 200 years old. Originally buried in St Peter's, in 1583 his remains were moved to the basilica of Santa Maria Maggiore. Feast day 30 April.

Pius VI *Giovanni Angelico Braschi, born Cesena 25 December 1717, elected 15 February 1775, died Valence, France, 29 August 1799.* The son of a noble family of the Romagna, he studied law at Ferrara, then entered the service of his uncle and went with him to Rome in 1740. There he became private secretary to Pope Benedict XIV and was made a canon of St Peter's, at which point he was ordained priest. He became in effect papal treasurer, and Clement XIV created Braschi cardinal in 1773 with the title of San Onofrio. His rule was marked by virulent anti-clericalism, secularism and atheism – with all of which he lacked the judgement and strength to deal effectively. He did, however, condemn the Enlightenment in his first encyclical letter, published on Christmas Day 1775. He dealt ineptly with Febronianism in Germany and Josephinism in Austria, but did finally condemn all Febronian teaching in the bull *Auctorem fidei* (1794). He was a considerable patron of the arts, and under his rule an effort was made to place the papal states on a better economic footing. The

French Revolution brought great problems; Pius condemned the Civil Constitution of the Clergy (1791), but also denounced the Declaration of the Rights of Man, and all the libertarian political ideals that inspired the Revolution. Bonaparte occupied the states of the church, and the Vatican had to surrender Ferrara, Bologna and the Romagna (1797). In 1798 General Berthier occupied Rome and declared it a republic; he took Pius prisoner and, despite his age and infirmity, drove him out of Italy across the Alps, until he finally died, still a prisoner, in south-east France. His heart was buried in Valence, but his other remains were taken back to Rome and buried in St Peter's.

Pius VII *Luigi Barnaba Chiaramonti, born Cesena 14 August 1742, elected 14 March 1800, died Rome 20 August 1823.* Chiaramonti was born into an old, but impoverished, noble family of the Romagna, and he became an oblate of the Benedictine monastery of Santa Maria del Monte, in Cesena, when he was nine, becoming a novice at 14: on his profession he took the name Gregorio. He studied in Rome, and was then sent to teach in Parma, coming back to Rome in 1775 on the accession of his relative Pius VI. Pius VI appointed him bishop of Tivoli – his openness to new ideas had caused some concern among his fellow professors – and then in 1785 cardinal and bishop of Imola. He was elected in Venice as a compromise candidate after a difficult conclave, and immediately made his way back to Rome. His main problem being relations with France, Pius proved conciliatory in his dealings with Napoleon, with whom he concluded a concordat which restored religion in France. In all his diplomatic activity Pius was assisted by Ercole Consalvi, the outstanding cardinal secretary of state. It was Consalvi who, as secretary to the conclave in Venice, had suggested Chiaramouti as a candidate. In

1804 Pius accepted Napoleon's invitation to consecrate him emperor in Paris. In 1805, Bonaparte occupied Ancona, despite Pius' protests; in 1808 a French army entered Rome and Pius refused to negotiate, upon which the papal states were incorporated into the French empire. When Pius excommunicated those responsible (*Quum memoranda*), he was deported to Grenoble, and imprisoned at Savona and then at Fontainebleau (1812). Released in 1814, following French defeats in Russia and Germany, Pius returned to Rome and, among his more notable acts, re-established the Jesuits, suppressed by Clement XIV in 1773; the Congress of Vienna restored the states of the Church. Buried in St Peter's.

Pius VIII *Francesco Saverio Castiglioni, born Cingoli 20 November 1761, elected 31 March 1829, died Rome 30 November 1830.* He trained as a canon lawyer in Bologna then in Rome, and served as vicar general in three different dioceses before being made bishop of Montalto in 1800, in which position he displayed great pastoral zeal. His refusal to take an oath of allegiance to Bonaparte in 1808 caused him to be exiled. He was created cardinal of Santa Maria in Transpontina in 1816, and bishop of Cesena, moving to the papal curia in Rome in 1821. He had the support of the conservative faction at his election to succeed Leo XII. Beset by chronic ill health, he nonetheless asserted his authority, and his first encyclical, *Traditi humilitati nostrae*, announced this intention, as well as to combat indifferentism, maintain marriage laws, and promote Christian education; he opposed secret societies, notably Freemasonry, in the subsequent *Litteris altero*. He effectively abolished the prohibition against charging interest on loans, hitherto condemned as usury. Buried in St Peter's.

Pius IX *blessed, Giovanni Maria Mastai Ferretti, born Senigallia, 13 May 1792, elected 16 June 1846, died Rome 7 February 1878.* From a moderately well-off family, he did not decide to become a priest until the age of 24, when he studied at the Jesuits' Roman College. He had thought of becoming a Jesuit, but instead looked after an orphanage before going on a diplomatic mission to Chile, which he regarded more as a missionary enterprise. He became bishop of Spoleto, and in 1832 of Imola, where he gained a reputation for liberal tendencies. Despite that he was named cardinal in 1840, and was elected pope on the fourth ballot. His predecessor's reactionary policies had alienated the Italian people, and Ferretti began well by granting a general amnesty of political prisoners and exiles, showing himself favourable to the movement of national unity. But his concessions came too late to satisfy the revolutionaries. In 1848 he had to flee Rome after his prime minster, Pellegrino Rossi, was assassinated. He left for Gaeta, where he joined Giacomo Antonelli, a cardinal from 1847 (though never a priest), who had left Rome earlier, and who remained his chief advisor until his death in 1876. Pius appealed to the Catholic European powers, and a French army occupied Rome in 1849. After his return from Gaeta in 1850 Pius abandoned his liberal attitude in politics, but the papal states revolted against the papal government and became part of the kingdom of Italy until, with the seizure of Rome by Victor Immanuel in 1870, he lost all temporal sovereignty. He refused to negotiate with the Italian government and became a 'prisoner in the Vatican'. Other endeavours, however, were more successful: he erected many new dioceses and missionary centres, he restored the hierarchy in England (1850) and in the Netherlands (1853); and his definition of the Immaculate Conception of the Blessed Virgin Mary (1854) stimulated

Catholic devotion. Great numbers of Catholics came on pilgrimage to Rome, and his plight (the 'Roman Question' in European politics) became a rallying-point for socially conservative forces. His *Syllabus errorum*, and the encyclical *Quanta cura*, supported the traditional beliefs of Catholicism by condemning various forms of modern thought and, indeed, modern civilization as a whole. The definition of papal infallibility by the First Vatican Council in 1870 increased the authority of the papacy, and more than compensated for the loss in temporal dominion that had marked his pontificate. Buried originally in Santa Maria Maggiore, his remains were moved in 1881 to San Lorenzo fuori le Mura. The funeral cortége was disrupted by an angry crowd which tried to throw Pius' body into the Tiber. Feast day 7 February.

Pius X *saint, Giuseppe Melchior Sarto, born at Riese, near Treviso, 2 June 1835, elected 4 August 1903, died Rome 20 August 1914.* Sarto came from a large family. He studied at the seminary in Padua, and became a parish priest, a canon of Treviso cathedral, bishop of Mantua in 1885, and cardinal patriarch of Venice in 1893. He succeeded Leo XIII in the last conclave where a veto was exercised – by the Austrian emperor against Leo's secretary of state, Cardinal Rampolla. He signified in his first encyclical, *E supremi apostolatus*, that his rule should be pastoral rather than political. However, political considerations forced themselves upon him, and he refused to compromise over the French proposal that, in separating Church and state (1905), the latter should control Church property. He thus secured independence from state interference, but at considerable cost to the French church. He also condemned Le Sillon, a democratic movement among young French Catholics. In the field of social policy, Pius laid down the principles of Catholic Action in *Il fermo proposito*, with the aim of restoring Christ within the home, the schools and society in general; social action and the labour question were integral to the total programme, but everything was to be done under the control of the bishops. He gave a lasting stimulus to the spiritual life of the faithful, and laid the foundations of the modern Liturgical Movement in his reform of the breviary, and in his *motu proprio*, which restored the Gregorian chant to its traditional place in the liturgy. On the other hand, the bitter battle over Modernism, and the condemnation of contemporary biblical studies, put back Catholic scholarship for at least a generation. Venerated as a saint in his lifetime, Pius XII canonized him in 1954. Buried in St Peter's. Feast day 21 August.

Pius XI *Ambrogio Damiano Achille Ratti, born Desio 31 May 1857, elected 6 February 1922, died Rome 10 February 1939.* Ratti studied in Milan before attending the Lombard College in Rome, where he gained a triple doctorate at the Gregorian University. He returned to Milan to teach in the seminary before being appointed as librarian of the Bibliotheca Ambrosiana in 1888. He also engaged in pastoral work at this time, as well as indulging in his hobby of mountaineering. In 1912 he was appointed to the Vatican library. In 1918, however, he was sent by Pope Benedict XV to Poland as Apostolic Visitor. He became nuncio when Poland was re-established. In 1921 he became archbishop of Milan, and a cardinal. He succeeded Benedict XV, and declared the chief objective of his pontificate to be the restoration of all things in Christ, symbolized in the institution of the feast of Christ the King. His great encyclicals have the same direction, and are landmarks in moral theology: *Divini illius magistri* deals with education; *Casti connubii* condemns contraception and seeks to restore a proper respect for married life; the best-known, *Quadragesimo anno*, extends the social teaching of Leo XIII. He supported Catholic Action in the encyclical *Ubi arcano* (1922). He settled the Roman Question with the Lateran Pacts of 1929. Although apparently sympathetic to Mussolini (and he certainly backed Mussolini's overseas expansionism), he nonetheless condemned the excesses of fascism in an encyclical of 1931. Again, though he entered a concordat with Hitler in 1933, negotiated by his secretary of state cardinal Pacelli, he condemned Nazism (1937), and, in the same year Bolshevism, and would have condemned anti-Semitism, had he not died before the encyclical he had prepared could be published. He encouraged the foreign missions, the need for native episcopates, and respect for the rites of eastern churches. He also sent aid to the starving in Russia, and attempted a mission there, although this ended in something of a fiasco. Buried in St Peter's.

Pius XII *Eugenio Maria Giuseppe Pacelli, born Rome 2 March 1876, elected 2 March 1939, died Rome 9 October 1958.* The Pacelli family was closely involved in the affairs of the holy see and, after his studies, all undertaken in Rome, Eugenio entered the Vatican's 'Foreign Office' while also teaching law in the academy for training Vatican diplomats. His first trip outside Italy was to the coronation of king George V. In 1917 he was sent as nuncio to Bavaria, and in 1920 also to Berlin. In 1929 he was named cardinal, and secretary of state. As such in 1933 he negotiated a concordat with Hitler, and spent much of the rest of the 1930s complaining about Nazi breaches of the agreement. He was elected to succeed Pius XI on the third ballot. Pius' first encyclical *Summi pontificatus* (1939) set out the principles that were to guide his pontificate: to restore to God his due place in the life of the world, and unity in defence of the natural law; his 'Christmas Allocution' enunciated the principles of a lasting peace in *Five Peace Points*. From the outbreak of the Second World War, he increased Catholic humanitarian assistance, and intervened without success for peace among nations; he condemned fascism and Nazism. In like manner he protested in vain against the fate of Catholics in communist countries after the war. He did not, however, speak out – or at least speak out clearly – against the persecution of Jews in Germany and in German-occupied countries, a failure for which he has been much criticized. Wishing to identify Christian doctrine in the modern world, he multiplied his speeches, media-diffused messages and encyclicals; he formalized the dogma of the Assumption of Mary in *Munificentissimus Deus*, and condemned Marxism, atheistic existentialism and the teaching of Freud. In *Divino afflante spiritu* of 1943 he gave encouragement to Catholic scriptural studies, largely in the doldrums since Pope Pius X's campaign against Modernism, and in *Mystici Corporis Christi* of the same year he expounded an ecclesiolgy of the church as the (mystical) body of Christ. In *Mediator Dei* (1947) he wrote a theology of the liturgy, and shortly afterwards carried out a number of liturgical reforms, especially of the Holy Week services. However, in 1950 the encyclical *Humani generis* attempted to rein in the theological speculation to which, to some extent, his own earlier encyclicals had given rise. He increased the number of native bishops in mission countries. He died at Castel Gandolfo. Buried in St Peter's.

Pontianus *saint, born Rome, elected 21 July 230, died Sardinia 28 September 235*. The son of Calpurnius; Eusebius says he reigned six years. Little else is known of his origins, or activities, except that he must have presided at the Roman synod of 230 which approved the condemnation of Origen by Demetrius, bishop of Alexandria. Exiled to the mines of Sardinia by Maximilian Thrax in

235, along with antipope Hippolytus, he died the same year of harsh treatment in the 'island of death'. The bodies of both were returned to Rome and buried by Pope Fabian in the catacombs of St Callistus. Feast day 19 August.

Romanus *born Gallese, elected end of July 897, deposed November the same year.* The son of a certain Constantine, he was archpriest of San Pietro in Vincoli at his election. Nothing is known of the circumstances of his election, nor of his short reign, nor of his death. A late account suggests he became a monk after being deposed. Buried in St Peter's (?).

Sabinian *born Blera, Tuscany, consecrated 13 September 604, died 22 February 606.* The son of Bonus, he had served as papal representative in Constantinople under Pope Gregory I, though Gregory thought him insufficiently firm on the issue of the controversial title 'ecumenical patriarch'. He then acted as a papal representative in Gaul. Little is known about his pontificate, though he improved the lighting in St Peter's. He incurred the anger of the people of Rome for selling grain in a time of famine, rather than giving it away as Gregory had done. Buried in St Peter's.

Sergius I *saint, born Palermo, elected 15 December 687, died 9 September 701.* He was of Syrian ancestry, studied in Rome, and became priest-in-charge of the church of Santa Susanna. He was elected on pope Conon's death after two other candidates, Paschal and Theodore, disputed the election between them. Sergius was the popular choice, and had the backing of the imperial representative. Sergius nonetheless soon clashed with the emperor Justinian II, who called a council in 692 without inviting any western bishops. It was concerned chiefly with disciplinary matters, but its decisions cut across western practice. Justinian persuaded the papal representative in Constantinople to sign the acts of the Council, but Sergius himself refused to do so, and when an imperial representative was sent either to extract a signature or to arrest the pope, the imperial army supported Sergius, and turned on the official, who had to be defended by Sergius. He showed considerable interest in the Church in England, and in the missionary work of Willibrord, making him archbishop of the Frisians. Sergius also concerned himself with the liturgy, improving the churches of Rome, adding the *Agnus Dei* to the liturgy, introducing processions for certain feasts, and beginning the celebration of the feast of the Exultation of the Cross. Buried in St Peter's. Feast day 8 September.

Sergius II *born Rome, elected January 844, died 27 January 847.* He had been brought up at the Lateran, and became priest of San Silvestro and eventually archpresbyter. He was an old man at his election, and the choice of the noble families at Rome after the people of the city had chosen someone else. He was consecrated without waiting for imperial approval, which angered the emperor Lothair, whose son Louis promptly came to Rome, devastating papal estates as he marched through them. At a synod in St Peter's the pope had to agree that in future no pope might be consecrated without imperial approval, and the presence of an imperial representative. In August 846 Muslim invaders ransacked St Peter's and St Paul's and this, combined with the open bribery and simony practised by the pope's brother Benedict, bishop of Albano, made him unpopular. Buried in St Peter's (?).

Sergius III *born Rome, elected 29 January 904, died September 911.* He was consecrated bishop of Caere by pope Formosus, against his will, he claimed, and was happy to be reduced back to the rank of deacon when Formosus' ordinations were declared invalid. He was ambitious to be pope himself, and already having a diocese was – as in the case of Formosus himself – technically a barrier to this. He was nonetheless elected to the papacy in 898, but was promptly deposed and driven into exile. Seven years later, in 904, when there was again a conflict over the succession, he marched on Rome, threw the antipope Christopher in gaol, had him murdered, and was re-elected by acclaim. He dated his pontificate, however, from 898. Sergius was backed by Roman nobles, including the influential Theophylact: it was later claimed that he had a child, the future John XI, by Marozia, the daughter of Theophylact. He once more nullified all the doings of Formosus and, in the east, approved of the fourth marriage of the emperor Leo VI, disregarding the canon law of the eastern church, and the patriarch of Constantinople's own opposition to the marriage. Declaring invalid all Formosus' acts, including his ordinations, caused immense confusion, and though hostile accounts of this pontificate come from the Formosan side, Sergius' actions ended the dispute. Buried in St Peter's.

Sergius IV *Peter Os Porci, born Rome, elected 31 July 1009, died 12 May 1012.* The son of a shoemaker, he changed his name so as not to be Pope Peter II. Otherwise, very little of note occurred during his pontificate, apart from the destruction of the Holy Sepulchre in Jerusalem in October 1009 by Caliph al-Hakim. He pursued a pro-German policy. Buried in St John Lateran.

Severinus *born Rome, consecrated 28 May 640, died 2 August the same year.* There was an almost two-year delay between Severinus's election and his consecration, because of his refusal to sign an imperial document endorsing the Monothelite heresy. While he waited, the papal treasury was plundered by the imperial representative in Italy, in order to pay his troops. Buried in St Peter's.

Silverius *saint, born Frosinone, consecrated 8 June 536, deposed 25 March 537, died island of Palmaria 2 December 537.* He was the son of Pope Hormisdas, and a subdeacon when he was forced upon a reluctant Rome by the last Ostrogothic king of Italy, and he had strong Ostrogothic sympathies. He was stripped of his office in March 537 by the Byzantine general Belisarius – who accused him of plotting with the Goths – so that the way would be open for the appointment of the deacon Vigilius, the empress Theodora's candidate. He was deported, but the emperor ordered him to be taken back to Rome to stand trial. Vigilius, now in office, had him deported again, this time to get from him a statement of his abdication. He died shortly afterwards, and is venerated for his sufferings for the orthodox faith – Theodora being a Monophysite. Buried on Palmaria.

Silvester *see* **Sylvester**

Simplicius *saint, born at Tivoli, elected 3 March 468, died 10 March 483.* The son of Costinus, his pontificate was largely concerned with an attempt to keep the eastern empire loyal to the decisions of the Council of Chalcedon of 451, under pope Leo, about the nature of Christ. The emperor Zeno and his patriarch Acacius were attempting, without technically breaching Chalcedon, to reunite the Monophysite (i.e. 'one nature') protagonists with the Chalcedonians. He reached an agreement with Odoacer, the German king who replaced the last Roman emperor in the west, that he should confirm the appointment of the bishop of Rome as the emperor had been accustomed to do, despite the fact that Odoacer was an Arian. In Rome itself Simplicius converted a public building for use as a church, the first known example of this. Buried in St Peter's. Feast day 10 March.

Siricius *saint, born Rome, elected pope December 384, died 26 November 399.* The son of Tiburcus, and a lector, then a deacon under Pope Damasus (as we know from a surviving epitaph, written at the time of his death), he was a popular choice as bishop of Rome, both among the people and with the emperor. He was firm and direct in government, issuing his decrees in the manner of an imperial official, to be binding in local churches in the west. His pontificate is taken to mark the beginning of papal legislation. Although he was a vigorous defender of orthodox doctrine, he criticized bishops who had condemned the heretic Priscillian to death. Buried in San Silvestro. Feast day 26 November.

Sisinnius *born Syria (?), consecrated 15 January 708, died 4 February the same year.* The son of John, a Syrian, nothing of significance is known about him. He died of gout. Buried in St Peter's.

Sixtus I *saint, born Rome, elected c. 116, died c. 125.* The son of someone called Pastor, nothing else is known about him, not even with certainty the dates of his pontificate. It is unclear whether he died as a martyr, as tradition suggests he did. Feast day 3 April.

Sixtus II *saint, born Greece (?), elected September 257, died Rome 6 August 258.* He was probably of Greek origin, and little is known of his pontificate except that he restored good relations with the church in Africa,

damaged by Pope Stephen I. He did this without sacrific-
ing his principles, for a letter has survived from Sixtus to
Dionysius of Alexandria defending the validity of baptism
administered by heretics. On the day of his death he was
dragged from the chair where he was sitting teaching, in
the cemetery of Praetextatus, and beheaded on the spot,
together with some of his attendant deacons. Buried originally in the cemetery of Callistus, his body was moved
in the ninth century to St Peter's, and later to San Sisto
Vecchio. Feast day 7 August.

Sixtus III *saint, born Rome, consecrated 31 July 432, died
Rome 10 August 440.* The son of someone also called
Sixtus (or Xystus), as a priest in Rome he was suspected
of having Pelagian sympathies. After his election his
chief concern, in the aftermath of the Council of Ephesus (431), was to reconcile warring factions without
betraying the decrees of the Council. In this he was
largely successful, as he was in maintaining for the most
part good relations with the patriarch of Constantinople,
without giving up papal claims, for example, to have
jurisdiction over the disputed area of Illyricum. He built
both Rome's first recorded monastery, and the basilica
of Santa Maria Maggiore, to celebrate the Council of
Ephesus and, in its iconography, to proclaim papal
authority. He also rebuilt, or refurbished, several other
major churches, restoring them after the barbarian invasion of the city. He was buried in one of these churches,
that of San Lorenzo on the Via Tiburtina. Feast day
28 March.

Sixtus IV *Francesco della Rovere, born Celle, near Savona,
21 July 1414, elected 9 August 1471, died Rome 13 August
1484.* The son of a wealthy Genovese cloth merchant,
he entered the Franciscans at Savona when only nine. As
a theologian he taught at a number of Italian universities

prior to his taking up various offices in his order, leading eventually to that of minister general in 1464. In September 1467 he was created cardinal with the title of San Pietro in Vincoli. His election to the papal office was relatively quick, a tribute to his reputation for probity. His policy was to bring reconciliation among the Italian states, but this fell apart when he backed the anti-Medici Pazzi conspiracy of 1478. Lorenzo de'Medici was excommunicated by Sixtus after an archbishop, who had been one of the plotters, was summarily hanged, and Florence itself put under an interdict. Unfortunately for Sixtus, the French and the kingdom of Naples backed the Florentines. But then a war broke out within the papal states itself, and even in the city of Rome, where the Colonnas, supported by Naples, battled it out with the Orisinis. When this war came to an end in 1484, Sixtus was left out of the peace negotiations. One of the most notorious of Renaissance nepotists, he raised six of his nephews to the Sacred College of Cardinals. In the cultural sphere, he refounded the Vatican library and is remembered as the builder of the Sistine Chapel, but he also engaged in the general embellishment of Rome, constructing several churches, the Ponte Sistino, and a number of thoroughfares. He approved the establishment of the Spanish Inquisition. Buried in St Peter's.

Sixtus V *Felice Peretti, born Montalto, near Ancona, 13 December 1520, elected 24 April 1585, died Rome 27 August 1590.* A farm labourer's son, he was educated by the Franciscans and, at 12, joined the order. He was ordained in 1547, and graduated as a doctor of theology at Fermo the following year. He was brought to Rome by the cardinal protector of the Franciscans largely because of his preaching ability, and came to the notice of Pope Paul IV. He was put on several commissions for the reform of the church, and was made an inquisitor, then bishop of Sant'Agata dei Goti in 1566. He became a cardinal in 1570 and bishop of Fermo in 1571. As pope he was eager to press ahead with reform – too eager in one respect: thinking that the reform of the Vulgate was going ahead too slowly he produced his own version, which had to be withdrawn. More importantly he reorganized the papal curia, setting up the system of 'Congregations' which still survives. This had the added bonus that it did away with the need for consistories, and possible challenges to papal authority. He also insisted that bishops should regularly report to Rome on the state of their sees, the *ad limina* visits. Politically he backed Catholic princes in their attempt to push back Lutheranism, but he was astute enough to recognize that Henry of Navarre was likely to win control of France, and therefore in his last years did not support Philip of Spain against him. He spent a great deal of money beautifying Rome and constructing new aqueducts, as well re-establishing the Vatican library and the Vatican printing press. The dome was erected on St Peter's during his pontificate. The money for all this he raised out of taxes and other sources in the papal states, which he ruthlessly reduced to order soon after his election, by executing thousands of brigands, and then by introducing financial reforms. None of this made him popular among the people of Rome, and a mob destroyed his statue on hearing of his death. Buried in Santa Maria Maggiore.

Soter *saint, born Fundi, in Campania, elected c. 166, died c. 174.* Born in the Campania, it is known he sent a gift to the church at Corinth, because a letter of thanks has survived. It was during his pontificate that Easter became an annual feast of the church, fixed as the Sunday following the fourteenth day of the (Jewish) month Nisan. It is common to celebrate Soter as a martyr, but there is no evidence that he was one. The place of his burial is uncertain. Feast day 22 April, suppressed in 1969.

Stephen I *saint, born Rome, elected 12 March 254, died Rome 2 August 257.* After becoming pope he was immediately called upon by the bishop of Lyons, Faustinus, to take action against Marcion, the bishop of Arles, who had become a follower of the schismatic, Novatus. He took no action and help was sought from Cyprian of Carthage, who in turn appealed to the pope, and it seems he complied. Stephen was also called on to intervene in another dispute arising from the Decian persecution, this time in Spain, where he declared two of those apparently guilty of apostasy to be restored to the church. In a later dispute with Cyprian he maintained, as against Cyprian, that those baptized in schismatic sects need not be rebaptized when they join the 'true church'. The *Liber Pontificalis* cites Stephen as suggesting that clergy should wear special clothes when engaged in liturgical celebrations. Buried originally in the cemetery of Callistus, his body was later moved to San Silvestro in Capite. However, Duke Cosimo III of Tuscany moved it in 1682 to the Cavalieri Chapel in Pisa. Feast day 2 August.

Stephen II *elected 22 or 23 March 752, died 25 or 26 March of the same year.* He had a stroke almost immediately after his election, and died shortly after that. As consecration, rather than election, was considered the beginning of a pontificate in the early Middle Ages, he was not regarded as a pope properly constituted. This was later reversed, but from 1961 he has no longer been listed among the popes in the official Vatican yearbook, the *Annuario Pontificio*. Hence the dual system of numbering of subsequent Stephens.

Stephen II (III) *born Rome, elected 25 March 752, died Rome 26 April 757.* He was an orphan and had been brought up in the Lateran after his wealthy father Constantine died. He served as a deacon, with special responsibility for the accommodation of pilgrims. He became pope following the death of the original pope Stephen II only four days after his election, and before his consecration. Because of the Lombard threat, under his pontificate ever closer alliances were forged between the papacy and the Carolingian dynasty – a fact that would influence the relations between the church and the kingdoms of western Europe for several centuries. Ravenna had already fallen to the Lombards, and when the Lombard king Aistulf besieged Rome Stephen, having exhausted all other methods, crossed the Alps to ask the assistance of the Frankish king, Pepin. This was agreed in early 754, and later that year Stephen crowned Pepin, forbade the French from choosing a king from any other family, and gave him the title 'Patrician of the Romans'. In 755 the Lombards were defeated and Stephen returned to Rome. But on New Year's Day 756 Aistulf attacked Rome, Pepin and his armies returned and the city was finally delivered from the Lombard threat. Stephen supported Aistulf's successor, Desiderius, in return for the restoration of certain cities, but these promises were not kept. Stephen corresponded with the emperor Constantine over the restoration of sacred images, restored many of the ancient churches and built a hospital for the poor near St Peter's. Buried in St Peter's.

Stephen III (IV) *born Sicily c. 720, elected pope 1 August 768, died 1 February 772.* A priest of Santa Cecilia, he was elected by a crowd in the forum after the expulsion of the usurper Constantine. He held a synod at the Lateran in 769 to ensure that laymen would no longer be eligible to elect or to be elected pope. This was to be reserved to the Roman clergy alone, a decision which irritated the Roman nobility, who were thus excluded from involvement in the choice of the city's bishop. The same synod confirmed the veneration of images, and anathematized the iconoclastic synod of 754. Through Stephen's support Leo was able to hold the see of Ravenna against a lay contender, and with the help of the Frankish kings some of the land taken by the Lombards was recovered. In the following years the pope was unable to prevent a marriage between Charlemagne and the daughter of Desiderius, the Lombard king. Stephen then allied himself with the Lombards, an unwise decision, because before his death the Franks and Lombards were once again enemies. Buried in St Peter's.

Stephen IV (V) *born Rome c. 770, elected 22 June 816, died 23 January 817.* He came from a particularly wealthy and distinguished family, which was to provide two more popes, Sergius II and Hadrian II. He had been set upon his clerical career by his father Marinus, who placed him in the Lateran for his education. He became a deacon under his predecessor, Pope Leo III. On his election he made the people of Rome swear fealty to the emperor Charlemagne's successor Louis the Pious, and went to Rheims in October to meet him. In the cathedral at Rheims he anointed (the first time this had been done) and crowned Louis, thus reinforcing papal claims to intervene in the succession to the imperial title. Pope and emperor had long discussions, apparently strengthening the bonds between the papacy and the Franks. Stephen died a few months after returning to Rome. Buried in St Peter's.

Stephen V (VI) *born Rome, elected September 885, died 14 September 891.* Born into a noble family, he served in the Lateran and became cardinal priest of the Quatro Coronati before his election by acclamation. He upset the emperor Charles the Fat by not awaiting his approval, but invited him to come to Rome, where Stephen was threatened both by internal squabbles and by threats from Saracen invaders. When Charles was overthrown, Stephen entered into discussion with those contending for the legacy of Charlemagne, but eventually threw in his lot with Guido, Count of Spoleto, whom he crowned emperor in 891. He also felt it necessary to maintain good relations with Constantinople, hoping for military assistance from the Byzantine emperor. In Moravia, where Methodius had died just at the time of his election, Stephen forbade the Slavonic liturgy, and the Moravian church was reorganized along German lines, driving Methodius' immediate disciples to Bulgaria, where they continued to develop the Slavonic liturgy. It was from here that Christianity penetrated Russia: Stephen's decision over Moravia, therefore, fundamentally affected the future development of Christianity in the east. Buried in St Peter's.

Stephen VI (VII) *born Rome, consecrated May 896, deposed and died August 897.* The son of a priest, John, he had been created bishop of Anagni by pope Formosus. As already a bishop, he was not supposed to accept the see of Rome. One way round this was to nullify Formosus' acts, which was done at the 'Synod of the Cadaver', when Formosus' dead body was put on trial, dressed in papal vestments and seated on a throne and, when found guilty, stripped and his body thrown into the Tiber. This macabre event so alienated the Roman people that Stephen was also soon after attacked, stripped of his insignia of office, and thrown into gaol, where he was strangled. Perhaps buried in St Peter's.

Stephen VII (VIII) *born Rome, elected January 929, died February 931.* The son of Teudemundus, which suggests German origins, he was priest of the church of Santa Anastasia. Nothing is recorded of his pontificate. Perhaps buried in St Peter's.

Stephen VIII (IX) *born Rome, elected 14 July 939, died October 942.* Cardinal priest of Saints Silvestro e Martino, he had very little independence, his appointment being at the wish of Alberic II, the effective ruler of Rome. They shared, however, a desire for monastic renewal, and an interest in the Cluniacs as the means thereto. It seems likely, however, that eventually Stephen conspired against Alberic, as a result of which he was put in prison, mutilated, and died there of his injuries. Buried in St Peter's.

Stephen IX (X) *Frederick, born the Ardennes, elected 2 August 1056, died Florence 29 March 1058.* The son of Duke Gozelon of Lotharingia, he was educated at Liège and became a canon, then archdeacon there before coming to Rome in the entourage of Pope Leo IX. He was one of the members of the fateful embassy to Constantinople in 1054, which resulted in the mutual excommunication of pope and patriarch. He entered the monastery of Monte Cassino in 1055, becoming abbot there two years later, and being appointed a cardinal. He was consulted about the choice of a successor to Pope Victor II – and was eventually chosen himself, though he remained abbot. As pope he was deeply concerned about improving the standards of clerical observance, bringing into the papal entourage others who shared his views, such as Peter Damian, whom he made a cardinal despite Peter's protests. In politics, he was determined to contain the Normans in southern Italy, and thought of employing his brother Godfrey, Duke of Lorraine, for this purpose, creating him emperor. He was in Florence to discuss these plans with Godfrey when he died. Buried in San Reparata, Florence, upon which the duomo was later built.

Sylvester I *saint, born Rome, elected 31 January 314, died 31 December 335.* Legend asserts that he baptized the emperor Constantine and that he was the recipient of the Donation of Constantine, an eighth-century document purporting to be a record of the emperor's conversion and profession of faith, and which allegedly granted wide temporal rights to Sylvester and his successors. Otherwise little is known of his life, though recognition of the primacy of the see of Rome increased during his period of office. He did not attend the Council of Nicea in 325 but was represented by two legates. There was a good deal of church-building in Rome during his pontificate, at the expense of the emperor Constantine. Buried at first in San Silvestro, but later moved to St Peter's. Feast day 31 December.

Sylvester II *Gerbert of Aurillac, born Aquitaine 940, elected 2 April 999, died Rome 12 May 1003.* He was educated by the Benedictines at Aurillac, was sent to Spain, came to Rome in 970, where he came to know the emperor Otto I, and later was a student, then master at the cathedral school in Reims. He became Archbishop of Reims in 991 – in circumstances which brought him into conflict with Pope John XV – and of Ravenna in 998, a year before becoming pope. He was highly regarded by the emperors Otto II and III, and owed all his appointments to the French kings or the German emperors, including the papacy. He chose the name Sylvester in full awareness that his predecessor of that name had been long regarded as the model of papal co-operation with the emperor. While the emperor would attempt to restore the empire itself, the pope would endeavour to restore the sanctity of the church. In fact Sylvester did much to realise this ideal, opposing simony and upholding clerical celibacy, and strengthening the Church in eastern Europe. The Romans, however, were unhappy under the governance of a Frenchman, and for a year the pope had to live outside the city, in Ravenna, though he died at the Lateran after Otto III marched on Rome. Buried in St John Lateran.

Sylvester III *John, born Rome, elected 20 January 1045, deposed December 1046, died mid-year 1063.* He was made pope when Benedict IX was deposed, but when Benedict himself resigned his office in favour of John Gratian, who took the name Gregory VI, Sylvester apparently did likewise. He then simply went back to being bishop of Sabina. Buried Sabina (?).

Symmachus *saint, born Rome (?), elected 22 November 498, died Rome 19 July 514.* Of Sardinian ancestry and a convert from paganism, he was supported by the clergy and the majority of the laity in opposition to the archpriest Laurence, favoured by the aristocratic laity, following the death of Pope Anastasius II. After a bloody struggle between the factions in Rome the candidacy of Symmachus was endorsed by the Arian king Theodoric on the grounds that he had been elected first, and by the great part of the community. He was elected probably because he was prepared to take a firm line against Constantinople, symbolized by his fixing the feast of Easter on 25 March in 501, rather than that produced by the system used in the east. After complaints were made against him to Theodoric he was summoned to Ravenna, having to borrow money to get there. En route, however, he discovered that a number of serious charges were to be laid against him, including debauchery, and he rushed back to Rome, where his rivals had taken over much of the city. A council was called, but two of Symmachus' supporters were killed on their way to it, including the father of Pope Agapitus. This council did not resolve the issues between Laurence and Symmachus, and another council was called. The problems eased, and Theodoric was persuaded to cease his support for Laurence. Later in his reign he opposed the Henoticon, supported by the emperor Zeno, as being contrary to the Catholic faith, and expelled the Manichaeans from Rome. He sent the pallium to Bishop Caesarius in Arles (the first bishopric outside Italy to receive the honour), and confirmed its primacy over the Gallican and Spanish churches. He introduced the singing of the Gloria (by bishops only) on Sundays and feast days, helped the poor, including those persecuted by the Arians, and embellished St Peter's and other churches in Rome. He built the first papal palace at the Vatican. Buried in St Peter's. Feast day 19 July.

Telesphorus *saint, elected c. 125, died c. 136.* The name suggests he was Greek, but little else is known about him, though it is possible that he died a martyr, and was buried on the Vatican, near St Peter's. Feast day 5 January, suppressed in 1969.

Theodore I *born Jerusalem, consecrated 24 November 642, died 14 May 649.* The son of a bishop, presumably of Jerusalem, he had possibly come to Rome as a refugee after the Arab invasions of Palestine and, as a Greek, was well-versed in the theological controversies of the time. The chief matter at issue was the number of wills in Christ – not an arcane argument because the belief that there was only one (Monothelitism) would imply that Christ was not fully human. The deposed patriarch of Constantinople, Pyrrhus, travelled to Rome to recant his belief in Monothelitism, and Theodore promptly recognized him as the lawful patriarch. But when he found that his recantation did not regain him his see, he withdrew it, and went off to the imperial court at Ravenna. Theodore excommunicated him. When the emperor tried to bring peace among the warring parties by producing a document (the 'Typos'), which simply insisted on the definitions of the first five councils and forbade any further discussion, the papal representative at Constantinople refused to sign and was exiled, and the office of the papal ambassador was closed. Theodore himself died before being presented with this document. Buried in St Peter's.

Theodore II *born Rome, elected and died in December 897.* The son of Photios, he was eager to bring back some stability to the Roman see. He recovered the body of pope Formosus from the Tiber, buried it with honour, and annulled the decisions of the 'Synod of the Cadaver' which had condemned the late Pope. Buried in St Peter's (?)

Urban I *saint, born Rome, elected 222, died 230.* Little is known of his pontificate. He is sometimes said to have been a martyr, but the Church of Rome was at peace during his time in office. Buried in the cemetery of Callistus. Feast day 25 May, suppressed in 1969.

Urban II *blessed, Eudes de Chatillon, born Chatillon-sur-Marne, c. 1042, elected 12 March 1088, died Rome 29 July 1099.* Of a noble family, he studied at Reims, under St Bruno, who afterwards became his most trusted adviser, and in 1070 entered the monastery of Cluny. He was called to Rome, where Pope Gregory VII made him cardinal bishop of Ostia in 1080. He was elected to the papacy at Terracina, near Gaeata, adhered to the

Gregorian reform – he had always been a firm supporter of pope Gregory VII – and sought ways to restore relations with the Byzantine church. He presided at the Council of Melfi (1089), which renewed the prohibitions against simony, lay investiture and the marriage of priests; at Piacenza (1095), he declared the ordinations of Clement III, the antipope, and his adherents, void and, in response to an appeal from the Byzantine emperor, Alexis I Commenus, called on Christian warriors to defend the eastern church. At Clermont, in the same year, Urban preached the first crusade, the most memorable achievement of his pontificate. However, if his success in preaching the crusade illustrated the remarkable recovery of the papacy, his vision of 'rapprochement' with Byzantium, and Church unity, was doomed to failure. The division was only reinforced with a stronger, more centralized government in the emergence of the Roman curia, and a growth in the influence of the College of Cardinals. Urban died before the news of the capture of Jerusalem by the crusaders could reach him. Buried in St Peter's. Feast day 29 July.

Urban III *Umberto Crivelli, born Milan, elected 25 November 1185, died Ferrara 20 October 1187.* Of an important Milanese family, he became a canon regular, then archdeacon of Bourges, and next of Milan before being made a cardinal, with the title of San Lorenzo in Damaso, in 1182, and finally archbishop of Milan (and office he retained during his pontificate) in January 1185. He was elected pope at Verona, and stayed there because of Roman hostility. He was antagonistic towards the emperor Frederick Barbarossa for largely family reasons, and refused to crown Frederick's son Henry as co-emperor. When this coronation was performed by the patriarch of Aquileia, he suspended him from office. He also refused to accept the common practice that, during a vacancy, the proceeds of a benefice should go to the crown. The final break came when he refused to accept Frederick's candidate for the bishopric of Trier and appointed his own. Frederick sent his son to invade the papal states, and managed to unite the majority of the German bishops behind his policy. Urban at first gave in, then changed his mind and proposed excommunicating Frederick, but the city of Verona decided they no longer wanted the pope on their territory. He was on his way to Ferrara when he died. Buried in the duomo of Ferrara.

Urban IV *Jacques Pantaléon, born Troyes, France, c. 1200, elected 29 August 1261, died Perugia 2 October 1264.* The son of a shoemaker, he studied in Paris, became archdeacon of Liège and came at the Council of Lyon in 1245 to the notice of Innocent IV who used him as a diplomat. In 1252 he became bishop of Verdun, and three years later patriarch of Jerusalem. He was not a cardinal when elected pope: there were only eight cardinals gathered in conclave at Viterbo, and they were so bitterly divided that they could not agree on a candidate from among themselves. One of Urban's first acts, therefore, was to create 14 more cardinals. He had to try to establish his authority in Rome. He succeeded in setting up a government there, but it was too insecure for him to move back to the city. His next concern was to regain control of the papal states, and to prevent Sicily falling into the hands of Manfred, the son of Emperor Frederick II. Urban's proposal was to offer Sicily to Charles of Anjou, who accepted. Manfred took up arms against the pope, who had to retreat into Orvieto, and then to Perugia, where he died. At the time of his death he was in discussions with the Byzantine emperor, Michael Palaeologus, who was anxious to prevent any renewed crusade against Constantinople and was prepared to this end to recognize papal authority. Buried originally in the duomo of Perugia, but his body was later moved to the church of San Lorenzo.

Urban V *blessed, Guillaume de Grimoard, born Grisac, France, 1310, elected 28 September 1362, died Avignon 19 December 1370.* He was the son of a nobleman, studied at Montpellier, became a Benedictine in Marseilles and then returned to Montpellier to teach canon law before becoming abbot of St Germain at Auxerre in 1352 and of St Victor at Marseilles in 1361. He was elected pope at Avignon, even though not a cardinal, while he was on a diplomatic visit to Italy, as a compromise candidate in a much-disputed election, the first choice having turned down the office. He was a moderate reformer, and in the papal palace lived a monastic lifestyle. In 1367 he returned the papal curia to Rome, taking up residence in the Vatican, the papal palace of the Lateran being uninhabitable. He was eager to forward the reunion of the churches of east and west, and was visited in Rome by the Byzantine emperor, though nothing further was achieved. He made efforts to rebuild Rome, including the Lateran, but unrest in Italy, and renewal of the war between England and France in 1370 forced his return to Avignon, where he died a couple of months after his arrival. At his own wish he died in the house of his brother, rather than in the papal palace. He was first buried in the church of St Marziale in Avignon but, again at his own wish, he was later reinterred in the abbey of St Victor in Marseilles. Feast day 19 December.

Urban VI *Bartolomeo Prignano, born Naples 1318 , elected 8 April 1378, died, possibly of poisoning, Rome 15 October 1389.* Bartolomeo, a canon lawyer, had been archbishop of, successively, Acerenza and, from 1377, Bari. He was a highly efficient, much-admired, papal civil servant, first at Avignon and then at Rome where he was head of the apostolic chancery. Though not a cardinal, he was hurriedly elected pope under pressure from the people of Rome for an Italian. He was a reformer, and called the cardinals to account for their manner of life. In August of 1378, French cardinals revolted, declaring the election was void because carried out under duress, and in September that year they elected Cardinal Robert of Geneva, who took the title Pope Clement VII. The vote was unanimous except for the three Italian cardinals, who abstained. Thus began the 39-year 'Great Schism' during which they were two, and sometimes three, rival claimants to the papacy. Urban VI's pontificate was marred by his undoubted instability of temperament, and by the violence which broke out in Italy, forcing Urban to seek refuge in five different cities in turn. Buried in St Peter's.

Urban VII *Giambattista Castagna, born Rome 4 August 1521, elected 15 September 1590, died 27 September the same year.* A doctor of law, and from a noble family, he had studied at Perugia, Padua and Bologna, entering the papal civil service as a lawyer. He was named archbishop of Rossano in 1553, and engaged on reform of his diocese. He attended the final session of the Council of Trent, served in the papal diplomatic service in Spain after resigning his diocese, was nuncio to Venice before becoming governor of Bologna, and an advisor to the Inquisition. He became a cardinal in December 1583 and was elected pope because of his pro-Spanish sympathies. He caught malaria the night after his election, and died before he was crowned. He left his fortune to a charitable confraternity at the church of Santa Maria sopra Minerva, where he was reburied in 1606, having first been interred in St Peter's.

Urban VIII *Maffeo Vincenzo Barberini, born Florence 5 April 1568, elected 6 August 1623, died Rome 29 July 1644.* Of an old Florentine merchant family, he studied with the Jesuits in Florence and then at the Roman College. He took a doctorate in canon law at Pisa then, thanks to the considerable fortune of his uncle, entered the papal service and rose rapidly through its ranks. He had the confidence of pope Clement VIII, who used him on diplomatic missions, and named him archbishop. He became a cardinal in 1606, while serving as nuncio in Paris, and finally, after a long, sweltering, contentious conclave, he was elected, by 50 out of 55 possible votes, to succeed Pope Gregory XV. Urban was vain, self-willed and extremely conscious of his position; he saw the papacy chiefly as a temporal principality, and made it his first care to render it formidable. He fortified the port of Città vecchia and strengthened the Castel Sant' Angelo, equipping it with cannon made from the bronze of the Pantheon, an act of vandalism to which the Romans attributed the epigram 'Quod non fecerunt barbari, fecit Barberini' ('What the barbarians did not do, Barberini did'). Among his ecclesiastical activities, he revised the breviary, rewriting many of the hymns himself, and the Church calendar; he canonized many saints, including Ignatius of Loyola, Elizabeth of Portugal, and Francis Borgia. It was Urban VIII who condemned the *Augustinus*, a work by Cornelius Jansenius, Bishop of Ypres, which thus began the long, drawn-out struggle over Jansenism. In 1627, he founded the College of the Propaganda for the education of missionaries. Under him Galileo Galilei, whose genius he acknowledged and whose personal friend he had been for years, was condemned for the second time, in 1633, and compelled to abjure. He was a considerable patron of the arts, who commissioned Bernini to work on St Peter's (finally consecrated by Urban in 1626) had other churches constructed by distinguished architects, and added a number of fountains, as well as other monuments, to Rome. He commissioned Bernini to construct his tomb. Urban was the last pope to practise nepotism on a grand scale. He failed to found a princely house, but he enriched his family to an extent that astonished even the Romans. He made a brother and two nephews cardinals, advanced other brothers, and enriched them all so exorbitantly that in old age he felt conscience-stricken. In his closing years, he allowed himself to be involved in a war over the papal fief of Castro, the result of which was a humiliating defeat which crippled the finances of the papal state. The Roman populace, already cruelly oppressed by his prodigal extravagance, broke into riotous jubilation at the news of his death. Buried in St Peter's.

Valentine *born Rome, elected August 827, died September the same year.* The son of a certain Leonzio who lived on the Via Lata, which was the wealthy, aristocratic area of the city. Beginning his clerical career at 25, he rose through the ranks to become archdeacon of Rome under Pope Paschal I. He was also close to Pope Eugenius II, but other than that very little is known about him, or of his brief pontificate of 40 days.

Victor I *saint, born Africa, elected bishop 189, died Rome 198.* The principal event of his pontificate, and an important step in the history of the papal supremacy, was the 'Quartodeciman' controversy, for the settlement of which he ordered synods to be held throughout Christendom. He himself assembled a Council at Rome, where he insisted that Polycrates of Ephesus, who had written to him in favour of the practice in Asia Minor, and other eastern bishops, conform to the Roman practice of keeping Easter only on Sunday, rather than on 14 (= quartodecima) Nisan, whatever the day of the week; though he threatened them with excommunication otherwise, it seems he was dissuaded from such severity by St Irenaeus and other bishops. Among other incidents of his pontificate, Victor deposed the presbyter Florinus for defending Valentinian doctrines, and excommunicated Theodotus, the founder of Dynamic Monarchianism. According to St Jerome, Victor was the first ecclesiastical authority to write in Latin, but it seems he wrote nothing but his encyclicals, which would have been published in both Latin and Greek, so this claim is doubtful. He was venerated as a martyr, but there is no evidence that he died of violence, nor is there any to confirm the *Liber Pontificalis* report that he was buried near St Peter in the Vatican. Feast day 28 July, suppressed in 1969.

Victor II *Gebhard of Dollnstein-Hirschberg, born Swabia c. 1018, appointed Mainz September 1054 (enthroned in Rome 13 August 1055), died Arezzo 28 July 1057.* A member of the royal family, from 1042 Gebhard was a very able bishop of Eichstätt and advisor to the emperor Henry III. He was named pope by Henry when a Roman delegation came to the imperial court asking for a new pope, but only agreed to accept a year later, when at Regensburg, and even then never gave up his bishopric of Eichstätt. He immediately set about a programme of reform: the choice of name indicated a break with the recent past and a return to the purity of the early church. Apart from reform, he was also preoccupied with the Norman presence in southern Italy, and went to Germany to seek the emperor's assistance. While he was there Henry died, leaving his infant son in the care of the pope. Victor had the boy's mother Agnes recognized as regent, and negotiated peace between Henry's family and potential threats to Henry IV. To strengthen his hold over central Italy, Victor made his brother abbot of Monte Cassino and a cardinal, but died shortly afterwards of fever while attending a synod in Arezzo. Buried at Santa Maria Rotunda, Ravenna.

Victor III *blessed, Daufer, born Benevento c. 1027, elected 24 May 1086, died Monte Cassino 16 September 1087.* He was a pious man, who had been a hermit, and a monk at Benevento (where he took as his religious name Desiderius) and then at Monte Cassino, where he became abbot, rebuilt the monastery, expanded its library and generally encouraged scholarship. He was made cardinal priest of Santa Cecilia in 1059, with responsibility for the monasteries in southern Italy. In his position as cardinal he undertook several diplomatic missions on behalf of the papacy, and was with Pope Gregory VII on his deathbed. He did not accept the papacy when elected, but retired to Monte Cassino and was only persuaded to take up the office a year later. He retained the abbacy of Monte Cassino throughout his papacy. Although consecrated in Rome, he was never able fully to establish control over the city. He held an important council at Benevento, which reiterated the main themes of the reforms of Gregory VII. He recommended Cardinal Eudes as his successor, duly elected as Pope Urban II. Buried originally at Monte Cassino, his remains were moved during the Second World War to the basilica of San Paolo fuori le Mura. Feast day 16 September.

Vigilius *born Rome, consecrated 29 March 537, died Syracuse, Sicily, 7 June 555.* He was born into the Roman nobility, became a deacon, and was named as successor by Boniface II – an uncanonical procedure which brought a storm of protest. He was sent instead to Constantinople as the papal representative, and while there secretly agreed with the empress Theodora that, in return for a guarantee of the papacy, he would reject the decision on the nature of Christ as agreed at the Council of Chalcedon. The Byzantine general Belisarius, possibly on the orders of Theodora, deposed pope Silverius and had Vigilius elected in his place. Vigilius, however, was not in a position to deliver his promises to Theodora, though he assured her, and the anti-Chalcedonian patriarch, that he shared their beliefs. He told the emperor Justinian the contrary, however. When Justinian wanted him to sign a condemnation of the 'Three Chapters', selections from the writings of three theologians Justinian judged to be Nestorian heretics opposed to Chalcedon, in the hope that this would encourage the Monophysites to accept the Council, Vigilius hesitated. Justinian had him seized while saying mass in November 545, and taken to Sicily and then to Constantinople, where he arrived in January 547. In April the following year he agreed to condemn the Three Chapters, and was himself excommunicated by some western bishops for doing so. When, however, Justinian reissued his condemnation of the Three Chapters in 551 Vigilius, still in Constantinople, protested. He was arrested, and fled across the Bosphorus to Chalcedon itself. Justinian now called a Council in Constantinople which condemned the Three Chapters and excommunicated Vigilius personally. Vigilius gave in, issued his own, required, condemnation, and after spending another year in the eastern capital, set out to return to Rome, but died on the way. Buried in San Silvestro.

Vitalian *saint, born Segni, consecrated 30 July 657, died Rome 27 January 672.* Upon his election Vitalian set about establishing good relations with Constantinople, trying to do so by evading the doctrinal issues which separated the two capitals and their bishops. The emperor Constans II was ready to respond, and even

came to Rome in July 663, the last Byzantine emperor
to do so. He did, however, also allow Ravenna to be a
see independent of Rome. When Constans was murdered in 668, Vitalian gave his endorsement to Constantine V, the late emperor's heir, rather than to a usurper,
a gesture the new emperor did not forget, backing
Vitalian's doctrinal position against his patriarch. It was
Vitalian who sent the Greek monk Theodore of Tarsus
to England as archbishop of Canterbury, and who
backed the effort in Northumbria to have the Roman,
rather than the Celtic, method of calculating the date
of Easter accepted in the Church in England. Buried in
St Peter's. Feast day 27 January.

Zacharias *saint, born San Severino, Calabria, elected
3 December 741, died Rome 22 or 23 March 752.* Nothing
is known of his early life other than that he was a Greek
by birth, and the last Greek pope. He appears to have
been on intimate terms with Gregory III, whom he
succeeded. A cultivated man, he translated Gregory's
Dialogues into Greek, and was noted for his political
adroitness and great personal persuasiveness. He
reversed his predecessor's policy toward the Lombards,
who were threatening Rome with invasion, and by
travelling to Ravenna, where the archbishop gave up his
hard-won independence of Rome, and to Pavia, where
he met king Luitbrand. He prevailed upon the king, and
later his successor, Rachis, to make peace with Rome
and to restore four captured cities. Rachis, however,
abdicated in favour of his brother Aistulf and entered a
monastery. Aistulf seized Ravenna, and was clearly
going to establish a united kingdom in Italy whatever
Zacharias might do, but the pope died before the
confrontation. In 751 he sanctioned the deposition of
the last Merovingian, Childeric III, in Pepin III's favour.
He held synods at Rome in 743 and 745; the latter

confirmed the condemnation of two heretics, Adalbert
and Clement, by St Boniface. He sought to persuade the
emperor in Byzantium to abandon his policy of supporting iconoclasm. Zacharias was an energetic and efficient
administrator who, as well as controlling the militia and
civil government of Rome, took an active interest in
the papal patrimonies. Buried in St Peter's. Feast day
15 March.

Zephyrinus *saint, born Rome, elected 199, died Rome
217.* He was born the son of a Roman, Halrundius, and
Eusebius records that he reigned for 18 or 19 years,
succeeding Pope Victor I. According to Hippolytus,
who became an antipope, Zephyrinus had little intelligence or strength of character, and the somewhat
important controversies on doctrine and discipline that
marked his pontificate are more appropriately associated
with Hippolytus himself, Callistus, his principle adviser,
and with his successor. Zephyrinus would not condemn
Monarchianism and Patripassianism, as Hippolytus
wished him to do. The statements Hippolytus attributes
to him are said to constitute the oldest recorded, dogmatic definition of a Roman bishop. There is no proof
of his martyrdom as alleged in the martyrology of St
Jerome, and his place of burial in the cemetery of Callistus is uncertain. Feast day 26 August, suppressed in 1969.

Zosimus *saint, born Rome (?), elected 18 March 417, died
Rome 26 December 418.* The *Liber Pontificalis* describes
him as 'of Greek origin, his father was Abram', which
seems to indicate Jewish ancestry, though nothing else is
known of his origins. He succeeded Pope Innocent I, to
whom he may have been recommended by St John
Chrysostom, and his election seems to have affronted a
part of the Roman clergy. He figured in two incidents of
note. (1) He granted to Patroclus, bishop of Arles, the

title of papal vicar in Gaul, and made him metropolitan of the provinces of Vienne and Narbonne. The bishops of Gaul resented this disturbance of their status quo, and Proculus of Marseilles went into schism. (2) In the Pelagian controversy, Pelagius and Caelestius, who had been condemned by pope Innocent I on the recommendation of the bishops in Africa, appealed to Zosimus, who absolved them as falsely accused. The African bishops were outraged, and told the pope so, who was then compelled to reverse his stand. He informed the Africans that he had not yet made up his mind but that, meanwhile, the decision of his predecessor was to stand. He took the occasion to read the Africans a lecture on the Roman primacy, reaffirming the tradition that the judgement of the apostolic see must not be disputed. In the event, the Africans appealed to Emperor Honorius, who condemned Pelagius, and in 418 Zosimus was obliged to issue at Carthage his *Epistola tractoria* condemning Pelagianism. Zosimus' fractious temper coloured all the controversies in which he took part, in Gaul, Africa and Italy, including Rome, where part of the clergy appealed to the court at Ravenna against him. He excommunicated them and would have gone further had he not died after a long illness. Buried originally in what is now San Lorenzo fuori le Mura, but his remains were later moved to San Silvestro in Capite. Feast day 26 December.

Glossary

Acacian schism: a schism between Rome and Constantinople which began under the Patriarch Acacius over the Henotikon (*q.v.*).

Adoptionism: the belief that the humanity of Christ was only the adoptive, and not the true, Son of God.

Albigensians or Cathars: adherents of the teaching that material things are evil, and that there are two opposing forces in creation. Good and evil which are, in some versions of the doctrine, equal and opposite.

Arian/Arianism: named after the Alexandrian priest Arius, who died in 336, Arianism in its basic form taught that the Son of God is not eternal.

Babylonia captivity: a term used for the period the Popes lived in Avignon, 1309–1378.

beatific vision: the vision of God vouchsafed to the redeemed after death.

Benedictines: monks following the Rule of St Benedict, drawn up in the middle of the sixth century.

Breviary: the book containing the prayers, scriptural readings, hymns etc. used by priests, monks and nuns in the Catholic Church.

bull: the name given to a particularly significant document issued by a pope.

Byzantium/Byzantines: Byzantium was the Greek city on which, in 330, the Emperor Constantine founded Constantinople (now Istanbul). It was the seat of the eastern Emperor until the mid-fifteenth century.

caesaropapism: in simple terms, the exercise of control by temporal rulers over the Church.

Camaldolese: an order of monks, founded in the early eleventh century, who combine eremetical (i.e., hermit-like) living with coenobitic (i.e., life in community).

camerlengo: the chamberlain of the papal court, and of the college of cardinals.

canon law: the law of the church.

canons/canons regular: canons are clergy attached to important, usually cathedral, churches, while canons regular live according to a rule, usually that of St Augustine.

Carbonari: a nineteenth-century secret society promoting the unification of Italy. The word means 'charcoal burners'.

Carthusians: an order founded in 1084 whose members live mainly in silence, each in a small house with a garden within the abbey.

catacomb: underground tunnels serving a burial places, usually used for those Christian ones in Rome, though there were others. They are often said to have been hiding places for Christians during persecution, but this was not the case.

Cathars see **Albigensians**.

Celestines: a form of Benedictine (*q.v.*) life, founded by Celestine V – hence the name – before he became pope.

Chalcedon: the city, opposite Constantinople, in which a council was held in 451 to settle several disputed questions about Christ. It declares that Christ is one person, but with two natures. The divine nature of Christ 'is of the same substance' as that of God, while his human nature is 'of the same substance' as humankind.

Cistercians: followers of a strict form of the Benedictine (*q.v.*) rule. The order takes it name from the abbey of Citeaux, where it was founded in 1098.

Cluny/Cluniacs: a monastery (and the monks following the rule of the monastery) founded near Mâcon in Burgundy at the beginning of the tenth century. Its reformed rule was followed by other monasteries, and had considerable influence.

conciliarism: the belief, held especially in the fifteenth century, that a Council of the Church has authority over the pope.

conclave: literally 'with a key' (*con clave*): the process of electing a pope during which the cardinals are locked in

consistory: a formal meeting of cardinals (usually) with the pope. From the middle ages to the late sixteenth century it had legal functions.

curia: the papal (or sometimes the episcopal) court, or administration.

decretals: papal letters with the force of law.

devotio moderna: (i.e., 'modern devotion') a form of spiritual life originating in what are now the Netherlands in late fourteenth century, emphasizing personal piety and meditation.

Dominicans: an order of friars founded by St Dominic in the early part of the thirteenth century. Their official name is the Order of Preachers.

Donatism: named after Donatus, bishop of Carthage; followers of this schism in the African church believed that for sacraments to be properly conferred, the minister must be holy, specifically he must himself not have handed over the sacred books to Roman authorities during persecutions, or must not have had his orders conferred by someone who had done so.

encyclical: a letter sent out by a bishop (most commonly in modern times by the bishop of Rome) to other churches.

Febronianism: a doctrine circulating in Germany in the eighteenth century insisting that papal claims had gone too far, and more authority had to be left to local churches – and indeed to the civil authorities. The author of the book making these claims, a Bishop von Hontheim, used the pseudonym Justinus Febronius.

filioque: the doctrine which insists that the Holy Spirit descends from the Father *and from the son* (= *filioque*). Though widely adopted, it was not part of the original fourth-century creed, or statement of faith, and was rejected by the Orthodox Church.

Franciscans: an order of friars founded by St Francis of Assisi in 1220.

Freemasonry: a secret society founded in the seventeenth or eighteenth centuries – depending on what one regards as its origins – which, at least in some forms, later developed a strong hostility to the Church. Catholics were banned from membership in 1738, a prohibition often repeated.

Gallicanism: a doctrine which argues for the more or less complete independence of national, specifically French – hence Gallican – churches from the authority of Rome. Though it could be said to have a long history, it was formulated in the Four Gallican Articles of 1682.

Henoticon: a formula proposed in 482 to reunite the Monophysites (*q.v.*) with the orthodox. It was backed by the emperor Zeno, but not accepted by Rome, and led to the Acacian schism (*q.v.*).

heresy: the rejection of a Catholic doctrine; to be distinguished from schism (*q.v.*).

holy see: the formal term for the pope and his curia (*q.v.*).

Huguenots: French Protestants.

Iconoclasm: the destruction, or at least the removal, of images (icons); the debate whether icons could be venerated convulsed the Greek church from the early eighth, to the mid-ninth centuries.

infallibility: the belief that the pope, when teaching formally a matter of faith or morals, cannot err.

indulgence: the remission, by the Church, of the punishment still due to sin, even though the sin itself has been forgiven

interdict: a punishment imposed usually by the pope either on individuals or even on whole cities or countries, banning those under it from taking part in religious services.

investiture contest: the dispute in the middle ages over the right of kings and emperors to bestow the symbols of office on churchmen – particularly bishops – thus giving them a degree of control over ecclesiastics.

Jansenism: teaching drawn from the *Augustinus*, a book by Cornelius Jansen, Bishop of Ypres, notable for its strict interpretation of morality.

Jesuits see **Society of Jesus**.

Josephinism: taking its name from the Emperor Joseph II at the end of the eighteenth century, it asserts the right of the civil authorities to limit papal power, and to reform the Church without reference to Rome.

Jubilee: an indulgence (*q.v.*) granted in specially denominated holy years to those who visit Rome and fulfil certain conditions. The first was held in 1300.

Knights Templar: a military order of knights founded in Jerusalem – their headquarters here in the Temple – c. 1120. It was suppressed finally in 1312 by the pope, under pressure from King Philip of France.

Lateran: a basilica, which is the cathedral church of Rome, and a papal palace, given to the Church in the early fourth century.

legate, papal: along with nuntius (or more commonly nuncio) another term for a papal ambassador.

Liber pontificalis: 'The book of the popes', an account of the lives of the popes, of most value for the early middle ages; some of the lives are contemporary accounts.

Macedonian heresy: the denial that the Holy Spirit is truly God; the name is taken, probably erroneously, from the late fourth-century Bishop Macedonius of Constantinople.

Manichaeism: founded by the Persian Mani, who lived during the mid part of the third century, it taught that there was a cosmic battle between two equal powers, good and evil or light and darkness. A Manichee's mission was to free the particles of light trapped in darkness. It had many similarities with Albigensianism (*q.v.*).

Marcionites: Marcion came to Rome in the mid second century, and there spread his belief that Christianity was about love rather than law, a stance which led him to reject the Old Testament, distinguishing the God of the Old Testament from the God of Jesus Christ.

missal: the book containing the prayers of the mass.

modernism: a movement at the end of the nineteenth and beginning of the twentieth centuries when scholars tried to apply scientific, or new philosophical, techniques to traditional doctrines and, perhaps especially, to scripture.

Monarchianism: adoptionism (*q.v.*) is a form of Monarchianism: an attempt to maintain the unity of God, as is Sabellianism (*q.v.*).

monarchical episcopate: the governance of the local church by an individual bishop, rather than by a group of elders (presbyters).

Monophysitism: the belief that there is only one nature in Christ, as contrasted with the definition arrived at during the council of Chalcedon (*q.v.*).

Monothelitism: the belief that there is only one will in Christ – a doctrine suggested as a means to reconcile Monophysites (*q.v.*) with the decrees of the council of Chalcedon (*q.v.*).

nepotism: bestowing offices on members of one's family.

Nestorianism: the doctrine that there are two separate natures in Christ, rejected by the council of Chalcedon (*q.v.*); it is named after Nestorius who became patriarch of Constantinople in 428, though how far he himself held the views attributed to him is disputed.

Norbertines or **Premonstatensians**: an order of canons regular (*q.v.*) founded by St Norbert at Premontré in 1120.

Novatianism: from Novatian, a Roman priest, who objected to the easy terms with which, it seemed to him, those who had lapsed from the faith during the Decian persecution in the mid third century were being allowed back into the Church.

nuncio or **nuntius** see **legate**.

Oratorians: a community of priests, founded in Rome by St Philip Neri: they were formally established in 1575.

pallium: a scarf-like garment, symbolic of the office of pope or archbishop.

Patarenes: a reform movement in Milan which appeared c. 1050, and which objected to lay intervention in ecclesiastical affairs.

patriarch/patriarchate: a title given in the early centuries to the (early) major bishoprics which had oversight of other dioceses surrounding them. In the sixteenth century it was extended to Moscow, and since then to other major bishoprics. The pope is 'patriarch of the west', and as a title of honour it is granted to the bishops of Lisbon and Venice.

patrimony of the holy see: the term used for church lands owned (under a variety of titles) by the bishopric of Rome, sometimes called the papal state.

patripassionism: the belief that God the Father also suffered in the sufferings of Christ.

Pelagianism: taking its name from a late fourth, early fifth-century British theologian teaching in Rome, Pelagius, the doctrine holds that an individual can take the initial steps to salvation by him or herself, without the need for grace.

Peter's Pence: a tax originally paid to Rome from the late eighth century by the English, though it was introduced elsewhere during the middle ages, and was revived particularly after the fall of Rome, and the isolation of the pope, in 1870.

Piarists: a teaching order of priests, founded in 1597 by Joseph Calasanctius.

Premonstratensions see **Norbertines**.

Priscillianism: a doctrine of strict asceticism and spiritual renewal derived from the teachings of a layman, Prsicillian, who c. 380 became bishop of Avila.

Quartodeciman controversy: some Christians celebrated Easter on the 14 (hence quartodeciman) day of the Jewish month of Nisan. This could be any days of the week, whereas in Rome Easter was celebrated on a Sunday

Quietism: the doctrine that, to be perfect, one must be completely passive in the hands of God – a teaching that, in its extreme form, renders traditional ascetical practices unnecessary.

Roman Martyrology: the official list of saints, arranged according to the day of their feast.

Sabellianism: deriving its name from Sabellius, a theologian of uncertain date, it is a form of Monarchianism (*q.v.*) that the persons of the Trinity were simply modes of divine action.

schism: separation from the unity of the Church, which does not of itself entail doctrinal differences, in which it is to be distinguished from heresy (*q.v.*).

schola cantorum: a body of trained singers of liturgical music, begun in Rome by Gregory I.

Semi-pelagianism: the doctrine that, although grace is necessary for salvation, human will alone is enough for the first steps.

simony: paying money for holy things, most commonly associated with the purchase of offices in the Church.

Society of Jesus: an order of priests founded by St Ignatius Loyola and which received official approval in 1540.

Theopaschite: the doctrine that, because God is united in the incarnate Christ, God suffers; this is distinguished from patripassionism (*q.v.*) which argues that the Father suffers.

Three chapters: a selection of writings from three theologians who were regarded as sympathetic to Nestorianism (*q.v.*), published by the Emperor Justinian in the hope of reconciling Monophysites (*q.v.*) with Chalcedon (*q.v.*).

Vulgate: the Latin text of the Bible as (mainly) translated from Hebrew and Greek by St Jerome at the end of the fourth century.